This collection of celebrity anecdotes – sometimes funny, sometimes scandalous – makes personal finance approachable and easily understandable. There's a lesson for everyone, whether you make $25,000 or $250,000.

— ANDY SERWER, Editor-in-Chief, *Yahoo Finance*, and former Managing Editor, *Fortune Magazine*

Whether you're a new grad just embarking on your financial life or a not-so-new one who simply never got your act together, Bobbi Rebell has amassed a list of to-dos that can get you on the right track without being overwhelming. Plus, it's a fun read.

— JEAN CHATZKY, Financial Editor, *NBC Today,* and Host, *HerMoney* (podcast)

Sure it is fun to play all day, but I think Peter Pan never wanted to grow up for another very good reason: there are no credit cards, mortgages, health insurance, or student loans in Neverland. In the real world, however, everyone struggles with these and other financial challenges. *How to Be a Financial Grownup* is the perfect personal finance storybook – with engaging money tales from real, successful people along with actionable advice. Follow their words of wisdom if you want a happy ending, folks!

— LAUREN YOUNG, Money Editor, Thomson Reuters, and former Personal Business Editor, *BusinessWeek,* and Senior Writer, *SmartMoney Magazine*

As a society, we're used to seeking health and lifestyle advice from celebrities. *How to Be a Financial Grownup* applies that approach to financial health – a critical but often overlooked component of overall wellness. The result is a collection of engaging, practically applicable lessons about money from a variety of worthy teachers.

— ELLIOT WEISSBLUTH, Founder and CEO, HighTower

To be a success, you need to know the difference between an idea and a gameplan. A lot of people have ideas, but not many have a real plan to bring them to life. Bobbi's book is full of successful people who've had a real gameplan. It's full of valuable advice to help make *you* a success – whether you're just starting out or looking to take your game to the next level.

— KENNY DICHTER, Founder and CEO, Wheels Up

HOW TO BE A
FINANCIAL GROWNUP

HOW TO BE A
FINANCIAL
GROWNUP

Proven Advice from High Achievers on How to Live Your Dreams and Have Financial Freedom

BOBBI REBELL

MAVEN HOUSE

Published by Maven House Press, 4 Snead Ct., Palmyra, VA 22963
610.883.7988, www.mavenhousepress.com, info@mavenhousepress.com

Special discounts on bulk quantities of Maven House Press books are available to corporations, professional associations, and other organizations. For details contact the publisher.

Cover photo by Claudio Marinesco. Makeup/hair style by Tonia Ciccone.

Library of Congress Control Number: 2016932955

Paperback ISBN: 978-1-938548-66-6
ePUB ISBN: 978-1-938548-67-3
ePDF ISBN: 978-1-938548-68-0
Kindle ISBN: 978-1-938548-69-7

Printed in the United States of America.

10 9 8 7 6 5 4 3 2 1

For Neil

CONTENTS

LIST OF FINANCIAL ROLE MODELS

Chapter 5: Investing Starts Now

Chapter 6: Family Matters

Chapter 7: Consider Your Real Estate Options

Chapter 8: Mixing Friends and Finances

Chapter 9: Wealth and Wellness

Chapter 10: Educate Yourself, Then Others

FOREWORD

THE CAREFREE AND UNBRIDLED JOY OF A CHILD is a beautiful thing. It's that enviable innocence that makes us smile. It's their rightful, age-appropriate ignorance of the world's challenges that allows us to revel in their happiness. Every child deserves this season of life, but as time goes on, if they don't grow up emotionally and intellectually – if they continue in their childhood ignorance – they will experience the full breadth of life's challenges. Contrary to popular belief, ignorance is not bliss. Ignorance is pain. And in the category of personal finance, ignorance can mean poverty.

Unfortunately, financial grownups are rare in our society (for a whole host of complex reasons). This is not meant to be a condescending statement. It's simply a fact of the state of affairs. Forty-six percent of Americans can't cover a $400 emergency expense.[1] Sadly, it's taking a toll on our physical, emotional, and relational selves.

A recent *Forbes* article came across my desk with a frightening title: "1 in 4 Americans Have PTSD-Like Symptoms from Financial Stress."[2] As someone whose life's work is committed to ending suffering, this makes me extremely frustrated. Frustrated because this is one area where people don't *have* to suffer. We are living in a time when all the tools and information you need to make wise

1. Tami Luhby, "76 Million Americans Are Struggling Financially or Just Getting By," *CNN Money,* 10 June 2016.
2. Kate Ashford, "1 in 4 Americans Have PTSD-Like Symptoms from Financial Stress," *Forbes,* 22 April 2016.

financial decisions are quite literally at your fingertips. So why are so many people stressed to the hilt?

Whether it's your mind, your body, your relationships, or your finances, it's rarely for lack of information that most people suffer, or stay in the rut of wanting to change but not being willing to do what it takes. Take weight loss, for example: There are more "how-to" diet books, supplements, and websites than ever, but over 50 percent of the U.S. population is considered overweight.

No matter the area of life, people suffer or don't make the shifts they want to because they have embraced damaging stories: false narratives about themselves or their circumstances that inform their personal identities. I was 30 pounds overweight in my twenties, and my story was "I am big-boned." Nonsense! There are no fat skeletons! The story was there as my excuse not to face the uncomfortable truth that I was simply fat.

When it comes to money and personal finance, I often hear stories like "I am not good with money," or "I am not a numbers person," or "money is evil," or "money is not a worthwhile area to focus on." These, too, are nonsense. Stories like these are the stumbling blocks of change. And most people feel the subconscious tension of wanting to change their circumstances, but the stories they cling to are taking over their minds like weeds choking out a garden.

When people want change in a specific area of life, the first thing I do is help them uncover the damaging stories they have been telling themselves. I want them to begin to question whether those stories are really true. Without shifting your story and embracing a new, empowering narrative, more information and tools won't create lasting change.

In the pages ahead, Bobbi has done a wonderful job of laying the groundwork for a new narrative for anyone willing to take the journey. If you picked up this book, it might be because you are sick of the story you've been telling yourself about money, and the time has come to make a shift. That's a great place to be, as frustration is a launch pad to change. Or maybe you are simply in a phase of life where the pages are blank and you get to write your own financial grownup story. Either way, this book is a great place to begin.

So as you turn the next page, consider what new story you will write for yourself that will empower you and propel you on the road to financial freedom.

Live with Passion!

TONY ROBBINS
Author of the #1 *New York Times*
Bestseller *Money: Master the Game* and
America's #1 Life and Business Strategist

PREFACE: STORY TIME

EVERY NIGHT my eight-year old son and I read a story before he goes to bed. Sometimes it gets us talking about his day. Or my day. Or what happened at school. Or something he's worried about. It starts a conversation. He asks questions, many that I can't answer. We talk more. And then he sleeps on it.

Stories do that. They get us talking. They help us pay attention to things that matter. They help us remember lessons. They help us relate to one another. They bring us together.

Stories are the foundation of *How to Be a Financial Grownup* because I believe that nothing grabs a reader's attention, and makes a lasting mark, like a compelling story.

When I started the process of asking successful people whom I admired about their experiences with money, I had no idea what to expect. What if they all said the same thing? That would make a terrible book. The project could easily crash and burn before it even got off the ground. Even worse, what if they didn't even want to participate?

As you'll see when you start to turn the pages, the very opposite happened. Each and every one of the extraordinary Role Models shared unique experiences. Who knew that a personal finance book would have stories that included a sex scandal, repeated battles with cancer, and tales of living out of a car? You'll read the incredible stories of Role Models who experienced these things and many more that will surprise you. Money is messy. Success is not a straight line to the top. Even the Role Models, some of the most successful people out there, have had their unexpected setbacks.

It was also important to be honest and transparent about the reality that we don't all begin at the same starting line. I believe that we can learn just as much from the born-rich Role Models, such as Ivanka Trump and Sir Martin Sorrell, as we can from the extraordinary rags-to-riches tale of a Role Model such as Tony Robbins, who at one point in his childhood didn't even have food to eat. Many a scion has blown their fortune or, even worse, lived an irrelevant life. The accomplishments of those who get a head start can be just as instructive and inspiring as those who start with nothing.

THE PROCESS

I wanted to make the interviews simple and fun for the Role Models, so I asked them just two questions:

- What was your financial grownup moment?
- What is the lesson from that, or one that you want to share?

A financial grownup moment is that moment when you realize that if you don't pay attention to money, you'll never have the financial freedom to live your dreams.

The questions were asked by different means. Some were in person, some were over the phone, and some were by email. I promised everyone that their contributions would be treated as quotes, and would be included in the book as is. No edits would be made without their consent, and even then would only be made in extreme circumstances. I gave no parameters. Some answers came in short and sweet. Some were a bit long. But they are all unedited and genuine.

The Role Models I selected to interview included a mix of business types. Some I had formed a connection with after interviewing them at Reuters. I looked for companies and individuals who had a strong interest in promoting financial literacy. Many were people whom I knew were doing extraordinary things in their fields, and I reached out to them even though we had no connections at all. Some were suggested by friends who then provided introductions. As the process went on I tried to hit a diverse range of industries and perspectives.

I then added a range of subject matter experts to give readers tangible information and advice for implementing the lessons. Like the Role Models, they were often people I knew from my years as a journalist, or they were experts I reached out to because they were leaders in their fields.

And of course I added my own perspectives, along with specific tips and ideas of my own.

No one was compensated in any way for participation in *How to Be a Financial Grownup,* and I wasn't paid in any way to include any person or company quoted or mentioned in the book. Every product, app, and website recommendation that I make is genuine.

My goal is to get you, my readers, to pay attention to your own financial story. And then you can take action and set a course that gives you the happy ending you desire.

CHAPTER ONE

BE A FINANCIAL GROWNUP

We ALL HAVE THAT FIRST MOMENT when we realize our parents aren't watching. The world is ours. We feel like we can do anything and they can't stop us. Odds are they won't even know what we did. Freedom at last.

Unfortunately, that exhilarating rush of possibility doesn't usually last. Eventually we are the grownups. Adult life is great – no one tells you what to do, what to eat, when to go to sleep, or how you can spend your money. But that's the problem – no one tells you. Now it's on you. And soon you realize that all the freedom you want often comes down to money.

Start to pay attention. You'll make bad decisions you'll regret, and you'll live with the consequences. You'll also make some great choices and enjoy the freedom that financial success will offer. Financial ignorance is the only true mistake, and it can be very expensive. So be a financial grownup.

IVANKA TRUMP

• ENTREPRENEUR

MY FINANCIAL GROWNUP MOMENT

At age 14, I remember waiting to board a flight at the airport with my mother and siblings. My mother gave me my boarding pass and I realized she was in first class and my brothers and I were in coach. With classic teenage angst, I expressed my displeasure at our seating arrangements. She told me that I was welcome to use my own money to upgrade my seat. She then reminded me that I should be grateful for the opportunity to travel at all. Obviously she was right and I flew to our destination in coach.

MY LESSON TO SHARE

Be judicious when deciding where and how to spend your money. I appreciate a splurge as much as anyone else, but I tend to be prudent more often than not. My financial philosophy is invest wisely and splurge selectively.

GET ALL THE ADVICE YOU CAN

A SIMPLE, MEMORABLE MOMENT from an impetuous teenager set the stage for Ivanka Trump to become a financial grownup. Most notably, someone who has achieved one of the ultimate marks of grownup success. Ivanka has become an independent entrepreneur and business leader, with her own identity, despite being the child of one of the most iconic, headline-grabbing businessmen and politicians in our lifetime – Donald Trump.

Ivanka learned early on that her parents' financial success was not hers. She had to make her own way. And when she did so, she could decide how to spend her money. Yes, she had a huge head start. But so do a lot of wealthy children. It would be hard to name many who have reached the levels of success of Ivanka Trump. She didn't just have a plan to be successful – she figured out how to execute it.

The vast majority of us have nowhere near the same advantages as Ivanka. But if we're lucky, we have parents with child-rearing philosophies like those of Ivana and Donald Trump, philosophies that instill solid financial values in us as we grow up. All the adult Trump kids are known to be solid, hard workers, and that's not always true of rich kids.

And as Ivanka points out so well, just because you have money doesn't mean you have to spend it. Taking her advice to invest wisely, and spend selectively, will carry you far.

Financial beginnings must not define who we will be as financial grownups. Some of the poorest children have become huge success stories. A great example is Tony Robbins, the uber-successful entrepreneur, speaker, and author of the best-selling book on finance, *Money: Master the Game,* who will share his financial grownup moment later in the book. Robbins has talked extensively about not having enough food when he was growing up. It doesn't get much worse than that. And yet he managed, at a very early age, to be a financial grownup. In his case it was because he had to. There wasn't room for excuses. He didn't have the financial or parental support that even the average kid has.

Ivanka and Tony are at opposite ends of the spectrum when it comes to their financial starting points. And yet they both achieved true financial grownup status because of their determination to control their financial lives. Your parents' financial success is not yours. Nor are their financial shortcomings. To be a financial grownup you must pay attention and take ownership of your own financial decisions.

Invest wisely and splurge selectively

To be clear – if your parents happen to be financially successful and that is a resource, consider yourself lucky. If they have the opportunity to give you a head start in life, such as paying for college, you're off to a great start. Don't be a martyr. Accept the help with gratitude and appreciation.

Get all the advice you can from adults who are willing to help out. If you have access to financial resources, be accepting. And if you don't, be resourceful. This book will help you make the most of what you have, or be successful despite what you don't have. Most of all, don't be afraid to ask.

KEVIN O'LEARY

- ENTREPRENEUR
- O'SHARES FOUNDER AND CHAIRMAN
- STAR AND INVESTOR, *SHARK TANK*

MY FINANCIAL GROWNUP MOMENT

My financial grownup moment came during my final year of high school when my stepfather, George, sat me down and asked me, "What do you want to do with your life?"

I told him that I didn't want to go to university. That I was going to be a photographer.

George proceeded to explain that "to be, or not to be" isn't the question. The question is: What are you willing to do in order to be what you want to be?

MY LESSON TO SHARE

If your dream is to become a photographer, writer, or artist, you have to be willing to make a lot of sacrifices to support that goal. I simply wasn't willing to take the risk of all the tasks and jobs required to support my dream of becoming a full-time photographer.

I wanted to make money, and lots of it.

Today, thanks to George's advice, I've built a successful career that allows me ample time and resources for my real passion – photography.

———

FOCUS ON YOUR FINANCES TO ACHIEVE YOUR DREAMS

KEVIN'S STORY ILLUSTRATES a common and costly myth that often prevents young people from achieving their dreams – the myth that following your passion will necessarily pay. If you really want to follow your passion, find a way to pay for it.

Following your dream doesn't necessarily mean that you should do that for income. It may mean finding a different way to pay for it, as Kevin does. And by the way, having interviewed Kevin a number of times and gotten to know him a bit, I can tell you that he's enjoying himself in the paying part of his career as well. Making money is a lot of fun for him.

Be willing to make sacrifices to support your goals

Being a financial grownup means proactively focusing on your finances. Doing a good-enough job will allow you to follow your passion. Later in the book you'll read some other stories of super-successful entrepreneurs who had passions that would never pay enough to be their primary source of income. Don't cry for them. By following a profitable and financially more-realistic path, they are now able to achieve their dreams. Kevin's co-star on Shark Tank, Mark Cuban, for example, is now the owner of the Dallas Mavericks. He's one of the most outspoken and passionate sports team owners out there. He achieved that dream by making money as a driven and relentless entrepreneur. Use money to achieve your real dreams.

There are, however, passions that can pay. Many people truly love what they do to make money.

Like Kevin, Sir Martin Sorrell, who heads WPP, the world's largest communications services group, also got advice as a teenager from an older mentor. His enthusiasm for the field of advertising is so strong that his passion and means of financial success did become one and the same.

SIR MARTIN SORRELL

• CEO, WPP

MY FINANCIAL GROWNUP MOMENT

I was 14 years old. My father used to run the radio and electrical retail division of a big industrial holding company, which was one of the first conglomerates in the U.K. He ran the retail division. Rather like Circuit City (That was!), but it had 750 stores throughout the U.K. And the guy who ran the holding company, which was an engineering company as well as retail, had a massive country house down in Sussex, I remember, near the White Cliffs of Dover. It was called Warninglid. We were at Warninglid walking around the estate and the man, whose name was Sir Charles Hayward, as he became known, said to me: "What do you want to do when you grow up?" (It was rather like The Graduate's "plastics moment.") And I said, "Please sir, I want to go into business." And he said, "Well, if you want to go into business you should go to Harvard Business School." And that sort of stuck in my mind.

Find something you enjoy

I was at Cambridge University in 1964, going to the Democratic National Convention in Atlantic City. It was the "Lyndon Johnson Coronation," as I called it. You had the poster outside the convention with the Barry Goldwater slogan saying "In Your Heart You Know He's Right." It was Goldwater against Lyndon Johnson one year after the terrible assassination of John F. Kennedy. And anyway we were there for the convention and the platform hearings in Washington, DC, and I decided that I would go up to Boston, while I was in the U.S. It was the year of the World's Fair as well, in New York. I decided I would go up to Boston and register my application for Harvard Business School, which I did in 1964, and received entry in 1966. And '66 to '68 I was there, so that was the moment of awakening. That was The Graduate Dustin Hoffman "plastics moment."

MY LESSON TO SHARE

My view is find something that you enjoy. The most important thing is to find something you enjoy doing from a career point of view. Not something that is work. In other words there is all this debate about work-life balance; I am not sure I buy that. Because if you can, find something that is almost like life, as opposed to work. In other words, a thing that you enjoy. So, for example, I worked for Mark McCormack, who founded and developed IMG and managed Arnold Palmer and Jack Nicklaus at the beginning. What he did is sort of exemplary of what I'm talking about. He was a scratch golfer. He was at Wake Forest. He met Arnold Palmer. He thought golfers needed professional advice so he thought: Wouldn't it be good – he was a lawyer – if he advised golfers like Arnold about golf and about their career. And since he was a scratch golfer it wasn't work for him. As he used to say, it was fun. So you find something that is fun where that division between work and life is not apparent. You develop a reputation in that industry, as my father used to say. It doesn't have to be a reputation such that Reuters would interview you. But you develop a reputation, you know, amongst peers, and then if you want to do something on your own, which I did when I was 40 years old (which was probably a little on the late side), you go out and start something on your own.

Don't be in a hurry. You know the conventional wisdom is to flit from flower to flower. You know, get experience in many companies. I disagree with that. I think you should build a reputation with one company, build a career with one company, then if you fancy doing something on your own, having got knowledge or a reputation in that industry or particular industry, then go ahead and do it. I'm biased because I'm trying to run a company and build long-term brands, but I think focus, rather than flitting, is probably the best.

FIND MENTORS AND ADVISORS

FIRST AND FOREMOST, Sir Martin Sorrell looked to older, more-experienced friends and family for advice when he was a teenager. He went on with his life, but he remembered that conversation from when he was just 14 and acted on it when the time came. He prioritized his education. Sorrell then focused on finding a career that was enjoyable, so that working hard didn't feel like working at all.

Having mentors and advisors is one of the best ways to become a financial grownup. Get advice from anyone who will give it. Ask a lot of questions. Be curious. I've done that my whole career, and in many ways Financial Grownup is the manifestation of that philosophy. I set out to bring you, my readers, the best advice from the most successful *Don't be in* people in a wide range of businesses. When *a hurry* I look at the list of incredible people who shared their experiences for this book, I can't help but smile. These folks had a million better things to do, but they took the time to tell their stories and give advice, in most cases simply because they were asked. So ask. Find someone you admire and talk to them about themselves. Most people enjoy sharing their experiences.

Use what you learn from their stories to stand on your own to make your own personal plan. That's the advice from Steve Lacy, who is expertly bringing media conglomerate Meredith Corporation into a new digital age with old-fashioned business smarts.

STEVE LACY

- CEO, MEREDITH CORPORATION

MY FINANCIAL GROWNUP MOMENT

I realized the need to develop a personal strategy when I was 33 years old and my first child was born.

MY LESSON TO SHARE

The critical path to becoming a "financial grownup" is self-sufficiency and education. No longer can employees – especially the upcoming millennial generation – rely on corporate America for long-term financial security and wellbeing. Each individual must take full advantage of educational opportunities to understand and carefully select their employee benefits and map a near- and longer-term plan for individual financial self-sufficiency.

The near-term plan for millennials would include elimination of student loans, management of their credit, and a savings plan for home ownership.

The longer-term plan would include family financial security around disability and life insurance needs, along with longer-term college and retirement savings plans.

IT'S TIME TO EDUCATE YOURSELF

S TEVE LACY'S POINT: It's on you. You must be responsible for your own financial planning. Your employer will not take care of that. But that same employer may provide a lot of tools and resources, such as tuition re-imbursement, matching your retirement savings in a 401(k) or similar savings vehicle, and subsidized insurance of all kinds.

Later you will hear from Role Model Bob Moritz who heads the U.S. firm of PwC. The auditing and consulting giant is leading the way on a new trend in employee benefits: helping to pay off student debt.

But you must know what you're entitled to, and proactively make sure you maximize those resources. Take the time to educate yourself. We live in a time when careers are cobbled together, and the path to success is more muddled than ever.

When it comes to investing, beware. What looks like a great investment vehicle may have hidden fees. Role Model Tony Robbins has talked extensively about the damage high fees in company-run 401(k)s have done to countless Americans' retirement plans. We'll talk more about that in the investing chapter, but some of the perfectly legal fees are alarming.

Reading the fine print is mandatory. I interviewed countless educated people in the housing bust who signed mortgages that were not what the so-called financial advisor verbally said they were. Then, when the loan became unaffordable, those advisors simply pointed to the contract the consumer had signed.

You are your own best advocate. Step up to the plate.

The Role Models in this book have one thing in common. They're all high-achieving, inspirational individuals who share a deep desire to help the next generation.

You will learn much from the Role Models in this book including:

- How to manage and pay off debt

- How to prioritize spending money

- How to balance the complicated relationship between friends and finance

- The best tools and resources to get started and continue investing

- How keeping healthy will pay off financially

- The best financial ways to approach where you live

- Strategic and savvy ways to manage your career

- Family matters and how they impact financial decisions

You will also benefit from a fantastic team of experts, in all of these fields, who have graciously lent their wisdom to this project. They all believe we need to do more to educate young people about finances.

I will also chime in with my own advice at times. I've learned a lot in my years as a financial journalist. I've also made almost every mistake in the book, and I continue to fumble my way along at times. In some ways this book came out of my own realization that whatever age or life stage we're at, we all need to pay more attention to our finances.

The title of this book was inspired by my friend and mentor Jack Doran. He was being promoted to a new and exciting job within Thomson Reuters, and it was my turn to move up and take over his old job running the day-to-day operations of the U.S. business video syndication group. I love being a journalist, but I wanted no part of management. I explained that to him. He looked me straight in the eye and said, "Bobbi, it's time to be the grownup." He went on to say that while I was terrific at reading a teleprompter, and could write a

You must be responsible for your own financial planning

script about almost any business topic in my sleep, I needed to accept the fact that it was time to come to terms with being an adult and the responsibilities that come with it.

And from that conversation came this book. I hope you find it inspiring, and that it motivates you to start approaching your financial life from a grownup perspective. Most of all, I hope you make the decisions that are right for you and that you use money to live your dreams.

CHAPTER TWO

A DEBT PRIMER

Y OU WILL NEVER BE A FINANCIAL GROWNUP if you have bad debt. Bad debt is anything that keeps you from being financially free. The most common is credit card debt. Student debt can also weigh down your life.

But there's also debt that can be used to give you financial freedom. Having a mortgage is often the most realistic way to own a home, which can provide financial stability. Most of us need to borrow to buy a car. Knowing the difference between good and bad debt, and how to manage both, is essential to being a financial grownup.

HEATHER THOMSON

- CEO, YUMMIE TUMMIE
- STAR OF *THE REAL HOUSEWIVES OF NEW YORK*

MY FINANCIAL GROWNUP MOMENT

Having credit card companies offer me credit lines as a freshman in college. Without an understanding of the interest rates, late fees, and over-the-limit fees, I got myself in a bit of trouble and had a quick reality check.

MY LESSON TO SHARE

There is no such thing as free money. Credit cards come at a cost. Unless you pay on time every month and use them to your benefit, they can be lethal. Read the fine print and don't use a credit card for credit, but rather to build it!

DEAL WITH YOUR DEBT

HEATHER HAD AN experience that's all too common. College campuses are jam-packed with representatives from credit card companies who make it as easy as possible for students to sign up for their first credit card. It's no surprise that a 2015 PwC survey found that more than half of young adults (53 percent) ages 23 to 35 carried a credit card balance in the last 12 months. In fact, young adults are so tight on cash that nearly 50 percent don't believe they could come up with $2,000 for an unexpected need within the next month. Living that tight is a recipe for financial disaster. Adding to

There's no such thing as free money

that recipe is the fact that, according to the same PwC survey, only 8 percent of the respondents demonstrated high financial literacy.

For many young people, their first credit card, and the bill that soon follows, is their first real exposure to adult financial issues, just like it was for Heather. A credit card sounds great – no more asking mom and dad for money. But the consequences of not getting debt under control are serious, so paying it down is the highest priority when it comes to becoming a financial grownup.

THE BEST WAY TO PAY DOWN DEBT

Credit.com's Gerri Detweiler, author of numerous books on debt has this advice:

Face Reality by Adding Up the Numbers

Getting a handle on your debt is the first and most essential step, but it's also one of the hardest. You probably have a rough idea of what you owe on each card, and know your minimum payments, but, as any credit counselor will tell you, many consumers significantly underestimate the amount of debt they owe.

If you haven't done so already, make a list of all your debts, including balances, interest rates, and monthly payments.

Be Realistic

Can you dig out on your own or do you need professional help? According to PwC, only 12 percent of young people seek help on debt management.

There is free help available. For example, you can use an online calculator, at many websites including credit.com, to see whether you can afford to pay off your cards in five years or less with what you're making now. You may also consider consolidating your various debts into one account. As always, do the math and figure out if that's the best move for your current situation.

But you may find yourself at a point where you need professional help. That's when it's a good idea to at least have a conversation with a credit counseling agency, or a fee-only Certified Financial Planner, to see what they may be able to offer.

Prioritize and Get It Done

Tackle the highest-interest-rate debt first. You make minimum payments on each one, except the most expensive one and when that's paid off you roll the payment down to the next one, and so on. This method will likely save you the most money.

Alternate option: If you're anxious to simplify your finances, you can knock out the card with the lowest balance first, and work your way up.

Either way can work, as long as you have a plan.

Change the Math

Talk to the people or companies that hold your debt, and make the case for lowering the interest rate. The lower your interest rates, the faster you will get out of debt, so it makes sense to try to get your interest rates down, either by negotiating with your current creditors, transferring balances, or with a debt-consolidation loan.

CREDIT SCORES: A GROWNUP FINANCIAL SCORECARD

Credit scores matter a lot. And with each generation the situation seems to be getting worse. According to Experian, Millennials as a generation have the lowest average credit scores compared to other generations, including Gen X and Baby Boomers. In large part that's because of the growing problem of student debt, which we'll come back to soon.

Part of the reason that young people's credit scores are so low, on a relative basis, is that young people simply aren't signing up for credit cards as much. Priorities are different by necessity. Young people are more focused on paying off student loans and, in some cases, buying cars. They don't have the track record to prove they can be counted on to pay off an unsecured loan.

NerdWallet found that about a third of young people ages 18 to 34 have never even applied for a credit card. That's a problem. To be a financial grownup you have to have credit. Yes, you can take out cash to pay for things. But if you want to get a mortgage, you need good credit. You also need a real credit history if you want to take out an auto loan. A good credit score will also help you get the best rates on insurance.

Not having a solid credit history can even hurt job seekers. Many employers check the credit history of job candidates. Someone with a low credit score could be perceived as irresponsible, unorganized, and, in some fields, even a security risk.

Which is why it's important to invest time when you're looking into getting credit, as told by the head of NerdWallet himself below.

TIM
CHEN

• CEO, NERDWALLET

MY FINANCIAL GROWNUP MOMENT

My biggest personal finance wake-up call came after my sister asked me to help her find a new credit card. I thought it would be a fairly simple exercise; as a financial analyst, I objectively evaluated dollars and cents as a living. It took me nearly a week to research and compile a spreadsheet of about 400 cards – a fraction of what's available in the U.S. – in order to make an informed decision. I was shocked.

Most Americans will sign up for a credit card at some point in life. If it took me – literally a trained professional – a week to objectively look at a sliver of what's available, how can any one person be expected to choose the right credit card for them? Or the right insurance policy? Or 401k plan? I realized the deck was completely stacked against consumers.

MY LESSON TO SHARE

My major takeaway was, Millennials are at the height of their financial confusion. They are faced with dozens of critical personal

23

finance decisions, and they need a trusted source of clarity around what to do.

The good news is, there is usually a "right" choice when it comes to personal finance. But depending on friends' and family's advice – or, even worse, signing up for a personal finance product because you got an offer in the mail that looked good – isn't going to get you the best product for your needs.

The biggest piece of advice I would give anyone is: stop being scared of, or apathetic toward, your money. Be proactive and look for simple, transparent guidance on how you should approach your financial decisions and select the best products for you. Taking a little extra time now can lead to millions down the line.

GET CONTROL OF YOUR CREDIT SCORE

NERDWALLET FOUND THAT many young people are in denial about the importance of having a track record when it comes to credit. There are so many horror stories of people getting into trouble for using credit in an irresponsible way during the great recession that it may seem better to just avoid it altogether. And grownup purchases such as mortgages seem a lifetime away.

But building a credit history takes time, and often the best time to start is in college. That's the time when companies will take a risk on a young person. Many will even give students a credit line without their parents as co-signers. Use the cards to make small purchases, and pay them off in full every month.

Another tip to boost your credit score: add up how much credit you have available. If you have three credit cards, and each has a limit of $1,000, you have $3,000 of credit available. Use only a small portion, ideally about 10 percent, and really try to use no more than 30 percent.

Stay aware of your credit score. Federal law mandates access to your credit score once a year, for free. A good place to start is www.annualcreditreport.com. All three credit agencies – Experian, Equifax, and TransUnion – make your annual reports available there. And though you can get your credit reports from all three agencies at once, you can also space out your reports and get one every four months. Know your number.

If you don't get a credit card in college, be strategic when you do apply. Every time you do, your credit score gets what's called a "hard" credit inquiry. The more cards you have, the riskier you look. That lowers your credit score and starts a downward cycle. NerdWallet advises Millennials to be patient and not to apply for a credit card more often than every six months, or even once a year. Also, research credit cards that are targeted toward the score you have, or toward new candidates with no score if that's your situation. And even if you're no longer in college, if you have a parent who will co-sign, by all means accept the help. Be appreciative and, most importantly, responsible. Now both of your credit scores are on the line.

There is usually a "right" choice

THE $1.3 BILLION ELEPHANT IN THE ROOM: STUDENT DEBT

Young adults are generally less materialistic than previous generations. Partly because there has been a cultural shift towards valuing experiences over acquiring material goods. But there's more to the story. Many also have so much student debt that they simply can't afford to engage in the old "Shop 'til you drop" sport enjoyed by many Gen Xers who grew up in the booming 1980s. Student debt has reached alarming levels, so it's no surprise that Experian found that student debt was a primary focus of young adults.

The Congressional Budget Office reports that student debt in this country is now at $1.3 billion. According to The Institute for College Access & Success (TICAS), the percentage of college students who graduate with debt had climbed to 71 percent in 2012. The average amount owed is $31,946, according to NerdWallet. There are a lot of reasons. One is that state budgets have been cut at many public colleges, so students who are looking for value in their educations, by going to the public system, are footing a bigger part of the bill. And the debt never goes away. Student loans cannot be discharged through bankruptcy.

Be Proactive, Informed, and Aggressive

Sara, a 23-year-old who recently completed a five-year masters degree in elementary education at a private college in New York, is laser-focused on paying down her student debt. The total cost of the program was more than $200,000. But she went into the process with her eyes open and made a conscious decision that this program would give her the right education to get a job when she graduated.

She started the process in high school by getting as many scholarships as possible. She received about $16,000 a year. She also knew she could count on some help from her parents. They paid as much as they could while she was in school. But they told her at the start that once she graduated, and her younger sister started college, their resources would shift, and she would be responsible for the rest of the debt.

Sara now has both a degree and the debt to go with it. A whopping $100,000.

The good news: her educational bet paid off and she got a great job, in her field, right away. After working at a day camp in the summer, she has started her new job teaching math to middle-school students. She's living at home and will put just about every penny she earns toward paying off her debt. She's also calculating the best way to pay, fully aware that there are different payment plan options and timetables that offer varying interest rates. Her lesson to young people: read the paperwork. There can be a lot of ways to save, even in the debt-repayment stage.

Student Debt Payoff Tips

Use direct deposit. Most lenders will shave about 0.25 percent off the interest rate if you do. Statistics show lenders that if the money comes to them automatically, it's more likely to get paid. Over the life of the loan that could save hundreds, even thousands, of dollars in interest rate payments.

Consolidate your loans. Sometimes lenders will bundle them all together. Not only does this make it easier to track everything, but you can often get a lower rate. Be sure to ask them to factor in a history of on-time payments as well as a good credit score.

Pay more often. Try paying every two weeks instead of once a month. You'll pay the equivalent of 13 months a year and knock down the total faster. By the way, this works with other debt, such as mortgages, as well!

Open Secret: Student Debt Can Sometimes Be Forgiven

Certified Financial Planner Cary Carbonaro, author of *The Money Queen's Guide,* shares a great new way to battle student debt. It's called Public Service Loan Forgiveness (PSLF). If you work in a public service job, your federal student loans may be at least partially forgiven after ten years. You have to be working full time in an eligible public service or nonprofit job, and you have to have made on-time payments. And it only applies to certain types of federal loans. But the Consumer Finance Protection Bureau (CFPB) has said that about a quarter of U.S. workers could be eligible. Jobs include teachers, social workers, and many non-profit workers, as well as those at government agencies and groups such as the Peace Corp. It's worth investigating.

Take a Close Look at Your Benefits

Companies are starting to offer to help young employees pay off their student debt. For example, PwC recently started offering its lower-level employees $1,200 a year to help pay down student debt. The benefit is good for six years and can help pay down a significant portion of the loan. One young employee I spoke with, Gabriella, was happy enough to have yoga and a gym. But with $30,000 in debt, the student loan perk was much more important.

As of now only about 3 percent of companies are offering this perk, according to the Society for Human Resource Management (SHRM), but as the job market tightens, it's likely to become an attractive way to entice young people who aren't all that impressed with ping pong tables and free food.

Leverage Online Tools

One of the many great things about the United States of America is that every problem seems to bring a wave of entrepreneurs looking to solve it. There are quite a few new websites popping up to help companies and their employees manage the repayment of student debt. Both Student Loan Hero and Flex395 owner Tuition.io have tools to help manage student debt, including ways to analyze the costs and benefits of different payment strategies. These can be valuable tools to help you stay on top of debt and informed about new ways to pay it off.

Up Your Income with a Side Hustle

The more you can earn, of course, the faster you can pay down debt. If you have the time, consider a side hustle. It's basically another job in addition to your primary source of income. It can be a way to earn more, gain new skills, or fulfill a creative interest. We'll talk more about it in the next chapter. Side hustles can be a great way to earn extra cash to help you knock out your student debt so you can get it over and done with.

This may seem obvious, but I'll mention it anyway – avoid taking on additional debt, which could distract you from paying down your student debt. That will likely mean putting off some purchases you want to make, even if retailers offer attractive financing. It may even be zero interest, but don't buy anything new if it means monthly payments.

Take a quick look on Craigslist. Find an item that isn't selling and ask if you can have it for free if no one buys it soon. Chat up the seller via email. Find out as much as you can. If it's a moving sale or they're redecorating and need the item out as soon as possible, tell them you will come and pick it up whenever they want. It may sound too good to be true, but it happens more often that you would believe.

On that note, someone you know is always redecorating or moving. Ask around. You'd be surprised how many people will be thrilled to give you something, especially furniture and old televisions, if you just come pick it up.

Which brings us to our next Role Model, legendary investor Elliot Weissbluth, and how he made a tough decision to say no to one of those no-money-down temptations when he was a young graduate.

ELLIOT WEISSBLUTH

• FOUNDER AND CEO, HIGHTOWER

MY FINANCIAL GROWNUP MOMENT

The summer after my freshman year of college I decided to buy a car. I walked into a dealership and learned that I had the option of financing one of their shiny new models by borrowing more money than I'd ever had in my life: no money down, just sign on the dotted line.

Tempted but skeptical, I looked at the interest rates and did some quick math. Yes, I could drive off the lot in a brand new car today and pay zero dollars out of my pocket. But the true, total cost of the payments and interest on the loan would have bought me *two* new cars on the spot. I turned around, walked out of the dealership, and bought a used Jeep instead – in cash. The Jeep needed a lot of work, but I realized I'd rather roll up my sleeves than rack up the debt.

MY LESSON TO SHARE

Using credit or loans to buy something you can't afford doesn't change the fact that you can't afford it. It only makes sense when the purchase delivers a return on your investment to offset the cost of the debt – like a home that will increase in value over time or an education that will boost your future earning power. Cars, on the other hand, start to lose value as soon as you drive them off the dealer's lot.

With a little elbow grease, my junker of a Jeep got me where I needed to go. More importantly, it steered me away from taking on an expensive debt burden early in my financial adulthood. Last but not least, that old Jeep introduced me to a new passion: to this day I still love to tinker under the hood of a car.

––––––

WHAT TO CONSIDER IN BUYING A CAR

ELLIOT'S PASSION FOR tinkering with cars is a great hobby. And it kept him out of the kind of trouble Heather Thomson faced early on. He thought about his priorities and his true needs. He also did not get emotional. We've all heard stories about people going in to buy a practical sedan and driving off the dealer's lot with a fancy sportscar. Clearly, you need to pay attention to what's really important to you.

Cars have always been a symbol of financial independence and freedom for young people. Countless movies and television ads have memorialized the ritual of a teenager getting his or her first car, and with it a taste of freedom from parents. In fact, in gathering these stories I was surprised at how often cars came up as being central to big life decisions. If your parents can buy you a car, debt free, count yourself lucky. But if you're on the hook to finance it yourself, consider your options carefully.

DO YOU REALLY NEED A CAR AT ALL?

New options have emerged in recent years that are changing the game. First and foremost, the sharing economy has come to the car business. Now, especially in urban areas where cars are seldom needed, there are lots of sharing options. They include short-term rental companies such as Zipcar as well as taxi-alternative services such as Uber and Lyft. So you may be able to avoid the entire problem of taking out a loan to buy a car.

Think carefully about whether you really need to spend money on owning a car, and if not, then just say no. You can always change your mind later if your needs change.

DO YOU NEED TO OWN THAT CAR?

Leasing has become much more popular among young people. According to Edmunds.com, the percentage of young people ages 18 to 34 who are leasing cars is up 46 percent over the last five years. In fact, in the first half of 2015 close to a third of all new car purchases were actually leases, according to Edmunds.com.

Edmunds.com found that Millennials were sticking to their budgets – doing the math and realizing that they could get a better car for the same payment by leasing. They are avoiding going into debt to own a depreciating asset, as Weissbluth points out.

The right car also changes with your life stage, and leasing avoids committing to the wrong car. The needs of a single person

33

are different from those of a couple, and a world away from the needs of a family. Leasing allows a lot more wiggle room as the picture changes.

I spoke to a number of the Edmunds.com survey respondents, and several told me that technology was a key reason they didn't want to own a car. Buying a car today and owning it for the life of the car, usually more than a decade, would put them far behind the curve as technology changed. Think about what the technology in a car bought in 2006 would look like in 2016. Connor, a young entrepreneur I spoke with, admits he will always have payments. But he also told me that he will always be in the car he wants to be in.

Allison, a 30-year-old executive assistant from Staten Island, also liked the lower payments of leasing, which allowed her to deploy the extra cash into other investments. In fact, she owns a couple of investment properties in the Pocono Mountains. It also got her into a higher-end car, specifically a Mercedes. She doesn't have to worry about repairs and enjoys having a new car every few years.

BUYING THE CAR

On a purely mathematical basis, buying has traditionally been proven to be the best choice. Most car loans are five years, and then you'll be payment-free for as long as you keep your vehicle. Loans are getting longer in order to lower the monthly payments. Doing that will ultimately make the car more expensive because you'll pay more in interest, but your lower monthly payments will help you meet other financial obligations such as paying down your student debt or having more money to invest. As of now, the average car on the road is more than 11 years old. So even if you stretch your car loan out a little longer, you'll have a nice stretch of years with no payments. And while cars do depreciate in value, when you do finally move on to your next car you'll likely get something for your old car, even if you give it to charity and get a nice tax deduction.

THE USED CAR OPTION

As I mention above, cars now last a really long time. And with all the leasing going on, there are going to be a lot more used cars available that are in great shape. So if you're looking for value, this may be an option. Don't be a snob.

Karl Brauer, senior director of insights and senior editor for Kelley Blue Book, points out that because car companies are going to have so many used cars to sell, they are improving their certified pre-owned programs. Warranties on used cars are as good as if not better than those on new cars. And he reminds buyers to always spend time researching before heading to the dealer. Given how much information is now available about the value of both new and used cars, there's no excuse to not be prepared and know what you should be paying.

GO FOR THE INTERNET SALESPERSON

The salespeople who work the floor of the dealership get paid on a traditional commission structure. They will assume that you haven't done extensive research online and will offer you a higher price from the start, according to TrueCar's Vice President of Industry Insights Eric Lyman. He says a little-known secret is that if you come in through the Internet sales team, they will often offer you a lower opening price because they know that you've done your homework. While it varies at different companies, Lyman says that in most cases the Internet sales team is paid differently and has more wiggle room when it comes to price negotiation.

GETTING THE BEST FINANCING

Here's a case where that good credit really hits home. Buyers with fair credit will end up spending about six times more to finance a vehicle – equal to about $6,100 in additional interest payments over the life of a $20,000, five-year loan – than consumers with excellent credit, according to WalletHub.

For all the effort car buyers make negotiating a price, they often let the financing slip through the cracks. Brauer says that the most important thing is to do your research before you even get to the dealer.

- Local credit unions often have the best deals. Banks can also have better rates than dealers.

- Make sure you know your credit score. Brauer says buyers are often surprised that their score isn't as high as they had thought and are left scrambling at the last minute at the dealer, figuring out if they can still afford the vehicle at a higher rate.

- Ask the dealer to beat, or at least match, the best rate. If they do, go with the dealer. They can make the whole process run more smoothly, without you having to go back and forth while the paperwork is being done. But if they don't, you will be prepared to take your business elsewhere.

- Don't relax. Watch all the numbers until the entire transaction is complete. Just because you negotiated a price for the car doesn't mean that you can put down your guard. Pay attention to everything. If you're trading in a car as well, fight for the best price. As it is you bought at retail and are selling at wholesale.

BEWARE THE UPSELL

If you're adding on extras, be careful that you really want them and that you aren't just becoming passive because you're excited to get your new car. Make sure that what's on the contract is what you agreed to. Read everything.

Brauer also says to really look carefully at the extras that dealers present. Take your time and do the math. In most cases paying ahead of time for things such as maintenance and extended warranties is not the best financial deal.

THE ULTIMATE GROWNUP DEBT: MORTGAGES

Taking out a mortgage is a really grownup thing to do. In many cases you're committing to payments that could last as long as 30 years. The amount of the mortgage is probably daunting. But take a deep breath. In general, mortgages are good debt. They allow you to invest in a home, which will likely be your biggest asset. We'll talk more about what to look for when it comes to deciding what to buy in Chapter 7 on real estate. But first, let's go over the key things to think about.

Choosing a Lender

The good news is that because of the Internet there are countless resources available. Try to choose a lender before you shop for a home so you're pre-approved. Get referrals from friends, and ask those friends why they had a good experience. Also ask them if there were things that they felt could have been done better. If you have a trusted real estate broker, that person can also make recommendations.

Ask a lot of questions before you sign on. Assuming you have good credit, lenders want your business. This is the time to negotiate, not when you're under pressure to get a loan to lock in a home you fell in love with.

Some good things to ask:

- What are the terms of the available loans and their interest rates?

- What are the title insurance fees?

- What are the fees for services you'll need such as help from an attorney and document preparation?

Get Pre-Approved

It may sound obvious but it needs to be said. Getting approved in advance can often mean the difference between getting the home of your dreams or watching someone better prepared snag it right out from under you. Get your paperwork in order. That will include pay stubs, W-2s, bank statements, tax returns, and relevant loan documents. It will help a lot to have locked in a lender you're happy with before going through the pre-approval process. If you want to switch lenders after pre-approval, you may have to go through the whole process again, which will involve another hard credit check. And as we know, that could hurt your credit score.

Do the Math and be Conservative

Don't take on a mortgage you aren't sure you can afford. There are a lot of adjustable rate loan products out there that can make your monthly mortgage payments lower. But beware. Taking on a complicated loan that changes rates after a few years is risky. If you have the capital saved to provide a cushion, it may work. If you know that you'll be moving before the rates adjust it could be a great option. But for most first-time home owners a conservative 15- or 30-year standard mortgage is a safe bet. Add up your housing costs. It should be no more than 30 percent of your income. Don't forget that housing costs include more than your mortgage. Factor in taxes, insurance, maintenance, and unexpected expenses, such as a large repair or a tree falling.

Read the Paperwork and Ask Questions

Taking out the biggest loan of your life is a big deal. Don't rush. You'll be on the hook for huge sums of money, and the folks you're dealing with are incentivized to get you to sign as fast as possible at the closing. Read through each page as you sign. If you don't like something, say something. Ask for clarification. If you still aren't happy, see if they can make an adjustment. Everyone at the table during a closing has a vested interest in getting a deal done that day. But if you need to stop and make a change, do it. No one else there is going to be living with the consequences of an oversight but you. They walk away with a check. You walk away with the debt. So make sure you do so with your eyes fully open.

YOUR FINANCIAL GROWNUP CHECKLIST
~ DEBT ~

- ✓ Don't be afraid to just say no when you're offered credit cards.
- ✓ Do be strategic and aggressive when paying off debt.
- ✓ Research ways to get help paying down student debt, from government programs to employers.
- ✓ Do the side hustle. More income from a second job is always good.
- ✓ Cars depreciate and are not investments. Do you really need one?
- ✓ A mortgage is probably the biggest loan of your life. Tread carefully.
- ✓ Always read the fine print. Twice.

CHAPTER THREE

CAREERS ARE FOR MAKING MONEY

THE MORE INCOME YOU HAVE, the more financial freedom you will have to do what you want. But we live in a society that celebrates doing something fulfilling. Imagine if colleges listed average salaries next to majors. Would the average student, about to take on heavy student debt loads, really choose a major that wouldn't allow them to ever pay their debt and be financially free?

But we're human. My dad's advice to me when I was growing up was to choose a career that paid a lot so I could do what I wanted, without worrying about money. We compromised on an internship when I was in college. I wanted to be a journalist. He wanted me to work on Wall Street, like he did. So I worked as an intern at CNN business news. I learned to be a broadcast journalist, and I learned about the financial markets. Fast forward and here I am. Find your compromise between doing what you love and what will allow you to pay for the life you want.

CYNTHIA ROWLEY

• FASHION DESIGNER

MY FINANCIAL GROWNUP MOMENT

When I was 21 and a student at the Art Institute of Chicago, a woman stopped me on the L-train and asked me whose jacket I was wearing. "It's mine," I said, "I'm a designer."

It turned out she was a buyer for a department store, and she asked me to come to her office first thing Monday with my collection. So I sewed like a maniac all weekend and made five pieces and brought it to her office.

The buyer looked at the first piece and said, "What's the style number on this?"

Deer in the headlights moment. "Uh, ONE?!"

"Okay, what's the style number on that one?"

"Um, two?"

She looked skeptical and said, "Where else do you sell?"

"Some of the more upscale mostly European . . . mumble mumble . . . boutiques . . . on Oak Street . . ." Throat clear. "Okay, I confess, I've never done this before but if you give me the order I promise I'll deliver a beautiful collection and you won't be disappointed." (a.k.a. fake it till you make it.)

I didn't realize I was supposed to ship to the warehouse and showed up at her office six weeks later – with the garments in a competitor's shopping bag. D'oh! But the collection sold out.

That was how I became a designer. I moved to New York, rented a loft, and a few months later held a show. The business went from that first department store sale of women's wear

Follow your gut, and take risks every day

to an international brand with 60 stores worldwide, and lines of shoes, handbags, surf and swimwear, fitness, eyewear, legwear, cosmetics, fragrance, and home furnishings.

MY LESSON TO SHARE

Lots of people encouraged me along the way. But I never looked for somebody to take me under their wing. There's no "right" way to be an entrepreneur. You have to have a vision of where you want to go, short-term and long-term, follow your gut, and take risks every day. It helps to be a pathological optimist and say yes to everything. The smartest thing I ever did was focus on the thing that most inspires and energizes me, and makes me excited to come to work every day. And no matter what the reviews are, never lose sight of the bottom line.

BUSINESS IS ALWAYS ABOUT THE BOTTOM LINE

THAT LAST BIT from Cynthia is key. Never lose sight of the bottom line. Cynthia Rowley may have taken risks, but she kept her eye on the prize – profits. Business is not a hobby. You're in it to make money. Rowley was optimistic, but she worked hard. She was ready enough when her big break came, and she had the guts to take chances and recover from mistakes along the way.

TALK TO STRANGERS AND BE NICE

You never know who is a possible business connection. By our very nature, people like to help people. I can't tell you how many people have been helpful to me in my career, with no obvious direct reward for them. Chat everyone up. Ask questions. Learn about other people's businesses and interests. They will often ask questions back, and in many cases they'll offer suggestions or introductions. Always offer to return the favor. The business world works on connections and mutually beneficial favors.

FOLLOW UP ON OPPORTUNITIES, IMMEDIATELY

Rowley may not have been prepared for that chance encounter, but she dropped everything to get that order done, and to get it done well. When someone offers to do something for you, say yes, and get to work. Do a really good job, and lock it in fast.

SAY THANK YOU EARLY AND OFTEN

Send all new contacts a follow-up email immediately. Connect on LinkedIn. If someone does something for you, send them a thank you email right away. Even better, send a token thank-you gift that makes a memorable impression.

I am partial to a local, family-owned business based in New York City called Treat House. They made customized rice krispy treats with the original Financial Grownup logo for me. I sent those treats as thank yous to the Role Models in this book. The notes I have received from the recipients have been fantastic. I hope those token gifts made clear my gratitude that they took the time to contribute to this project.

Always send to the VIP, the decision-maker, and the team. Most people don't. Getting the team on your side is not only a smart move in the short term, it also creates a base at that company even if your main point of contact moves on to another job. It's also a nice thing to do and makes people feel happy and appreciated.

TO REPEAT, BUSINESS IS ABOUT MAKING MONEY

Cynthia Rowley was realistic about the upside of her business and, most importantly, chose a field where she was talented and could make money. That's not always the case.

CHARLES BEST

• CEO, DONORSCHOOSE.ORG

MY FINANCIAL GROWNUP MOMENT

I've been a fan of bass fishing for as long as I can remember. In the sixth grade I planned to start my own business making custom fishing lures. I researched all of the costs for my tiny venture – from the molds and molten lead I'd need to make the lure weights, to the classified ads I'd need to promote my product in *Bassmaster Magazine*. This was before Amazon, Etsy, or Kickstarter ever existed. Ultimately I realized that the start-up costs and the number of lures I'd have to sell to recoup my investment were too much. Instead I became a soccer referee to make some cash.

MY LESSON TO SHARE

The most incredible businesses are started by entrepreneurs who relentlessly pursue their passion, but passion works best with a thoughtful, ambitious-yet-grounded business plan.

WEIGH PASSION VS. PROFITABILITY

C HARLES BEST MAKES a great point, and it ties into Cynthia Rowley's business philosophy. We all want to follow our passion. We want to make money at what we're really good at or what we enjoy doing. But that doesn't always mean the market will reward us financially for that skill or hobby. It just may not be the career or business that will help us achieve our goals, which should include being financially successful. There's a big difference between a passion that makes a great hobby and one that will lead to financial stability and freedom.

DON'T BELIEVE THE HYPE

We have been indoctrinated by years of seeing those commercials and news reports where someone ditched the high-pressure Wall Street banking job in order to follow their passion for something artistic and fun, like making cupcakes. Or artisanal beer. Or becoming a farmer. And it may be true that that person is happier leaving behind the pressures of

Passion works best with a thoughtful business plan

that high-stress job. But there's a lot left unsaid in that beautifully-shot, 30- or 60-second ad or 3-minute news report.

First, if the person really did spend 20 years in a miserable and demanding but lucrative job, odds are they've amassed a huge financial cushion. They had the resources, education, and capital to start the bakery or other adorable small business they now run. And while in this aspirational world they love being up at the crack of dawn to bake cupcakes seven days a week (if you believe the glorified story that they're always hands-on like that), the reality is that they are up at the crack of dawn, seven days a week.

GO IN WITH YOUR EYES OPEN

The lower income these entrepreneurs now make is romanticized because now they're in control. But they're also now dealing with the incredible demands of a small business, which includes employees, payroll, inventory, supplies, rent, price pressures, and all the various challenges of growing a business. It could have been the best choice in the world for them, but stress-free it's not. And, for a while at least, it's probably also not that lucrative. Not everyone can execute a startup. Be realistic about your ability.

Starting your own business can be a great idea, but, as Charles Best points out, it must be thoughtfully researched and grounded in reality. Whether it's custom fishing lures or turning grandma's recipe into the next big thing, be deliberate and measured in your approach. Go in with your eyes open.

BE WELL CAPITALIZED

Serial entrepreneur Shari Schneider learned the hard way.

She had success early on with two wine bars (called Divine Bar) in New York City in the early 2000s when Wall Street was booming. But then she wanted to expand into restaurants. She signed a lease for a prime location on New York City's Upper West Side. But she didn't anticipate all the red tape involved. Her opening was delayed, and her costs soared. When she finally opened for business, she had a great restaurant and lots of community support. The place was packed. Anyone who came to eat would have thought she was rolling in cash. But financially she was already behind the eight ball. Her business folded within a year.

So if you're going to start a business, make sure that you have enough capital to last much longer than you expect. Anticipate not only little revenue but high costs as well, such as rent and construction.

Also make sure there's a clear need for your business. While this was not Schneider's primary challenge, it didn't help that there were plenty of other restaurants around. Finding a niche that's just emerging is a great way to gain traction right from the get go. That was the case of Betterment CEO Jon Stein, who seized on the need for more-automated investment advice when he conceived his robo-advisory business, Betterment.

JON STEIN

• CEO, BETTERMENT

MY FINANCIAL GROWNUP MOMENT

When I graduated and started earning real money, I quickly became a financial grownup. It was my money, and I wanted to manage it well. So I pored over research and strategies to optimize. I was disappointed that no obvious best, low-maintenance, low-cost solution existed.

MY LESSON TO SHARE

Build a more aggressive, longer-term vision. Be confident in your abilities and paint the picture of the future you want to see. There are millions of people out there just like you, looking for this product.

BE A FIRST MOVER

Jon Stein's sentiment is right on track. Countless successful businesses have been started because the founders themselves needed the product. And he's right. It generally only gets harder to start a business as you get older and have more responsibilities. And while doing the right research is important, the clock ticks loudly on the best ideas. The first mover doesn't always win, but letting someone else get a head start is generally a bad move.

And that brings us to Dottie Herman, a dynamic and inspiring titan in the real estate world who made her move against all odds. Her story is incredible.

Build a more aggressive, longer-term vision

DOTTIE HERMAN

• CEO, DOUGLAS ELLIMAN

MY FINANCIAL GROWNUP MOMENT

Merrill Lynch ruled the real estate world in the 1980s, and I was lucky to be a part of it. It was exhilarating, fun, and empowering. I got as much as I gave, learning and earning along the way. But that part of my life came to an abrupt end when the global giant decided to put their real estate division on the market.

However, for me, my business life was really just beginning.

I was temporarily tasked with keeping Merrill's 36 offices on Long Island and Queens percolating until a buyer could be found. A year later, along came Prudential to buy Merrill's real estate division. Prudential, however, did not want to own a national real estate business. Prudential felt real estate was strictly a local affair.

A colleague with some chutzpah whispered in my ear: buy it! Send them a letter saying you have venture capital money, even if you don't! Talk about chutzpah! The brazen friend said not to worry. You will find someone to lend you the money. I was young and not fearful of failure. I thirsted for a challenge.

The banks, of course, turned me down. I was not deterred. I turned to Prudential executives themselves and asked if they would finance me. No, they said. They could not do that. These door-slams just made me more determined than ever. I took the ball and ran with it. I stood before 1,600 real estate agents

Taking no for an answer is never an option

and asked them to stand by me, to send letters to Prudential asking that they back me. I am pleased to say they did as I asked.

Along with some attorneys and successful business people, I put together a business plan that stood up to Prudential's tough standards. Prudential gave me a loan of about $7 million and $1.7 million in capital. I guess I was a born salesperson. I got the money and capital with no money down and no guarantee. I have been blessed, I have done well. So has Prudential, and so have my many loyal employees and clients.

MY LESSON TO SHARE

If this all sounds like a fairy tale, I am here to tell you it's all the God's honest truth. I am living proof that taking no for an answer is never an option. When I am asked what advice I give to young people, I have a simple answer: don't be afraid of the word no, and don't be afraid to fail. Success, after all, is failure turned inside out.

GO FOR THE YES

Like Dottie, the most successful people are often told no over and over. Keep at it, and go for the yes. When I made my dream list of Role Models for this book, many people close to me had their doubts. But I went for the yes, was persistent, and the results speak for themselves. I didn't have anything to offer the Role Models in return. I just asked. Sometimes repeatedly. Always nicely. But I went for the yes. You should, too.

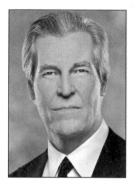

TERRY LUNDGREN

• CHAIRMAN AND CEO, MACY'S, INC.

MY FINANCIAL GROWNUP MOMENT

I had graduated college and I was lucky enough to have had several job offers. And at that point in my life, since I had paid for college myself, I was completely broke. And I just wanted a car that would guarantee getting me to and from each point I intended to get to and from. I had a broken-down Volkswagen bug that would occasionally start – but not always. So I really wanted a new car, and I was highly motivated by the highest-paying job. That was Xerox. I got the offer from them. I had basically agreed verbally that I was going to take that job offer. And it was me and about 13 other people who looked just like me, and dressed just like me, and were coming out of school. It felt like we were getting a group offer. But the most important thing was that it was the highest-paying job. So that was my motivation.

And then two days later, Bullock's department store in Los Angeles was offering to fly me there from my college, which was the University of Arizona, for an interview. And I said, well, what the heck. I'll go anyway, because you know it's a free weekend in

California, where I grew up. So I'm going to take that opportunity. But I had basically made up my mind (to accept the Xerox offer).

When I went through the interview process at Bullock's I was completely blown away and really impressed with the time they took to treat me like an individual. And, long story short, they made me an offer that, at least in my mind, seemed quite a bit lower than the Xerox offer. I told them I just couldn't take it because I really did need to buy a new car!

So they ended up convincing me to take that job offer. They did sweeten the pot a little bit. But

Have a long-term perspective

still a lot lower than the Xerox offer. But what they said was: "Well look, you just said that we paid more attention to you. You get to experience how personal we are, and if you do well people are going to notice you at this company. If you don't think you've made the right decision then six months later, go work for Xerox, or go work for someone else, but you will regret not having tried this out for at least six months." And I said, "You know what? I'm going to take you up on that." I took the job and six months later that college recruiter from the HR office said, "So it's been six months; what do you think?" And I said, "I need another six months because I love what I am doing!"

Long story short: Within 13 years I was president of the company. So I clearly was thinking about money first, as opposed to a career company where I would be a good fit, and where people were paying attention to me, and where I thought if I performed well I would have a chance to break out of the pack and have a great career. I think that turned out to be a good decision.

MY LESSON TO SHARE

I think the lesson is to think a little bit longer-term than the next six months. I think the lesson has been for me to think about where I might imagine myself in the future, and I would do the same thing today. Even in challenging times in business, I try to imagine what the business should look like a year from now, and what steps we need to take between now and then to achieve that vision. So I think just having a longer-term perspective is the lesson that I took away from that experience.

ADVANTAGES TO GOING CORPORATE

Terry was laser-focused on instantly earning money. So he chose the corporate route, and, given his success, that has clearly been a great decision. But he was strategic in his choice. He made sure to position himself where he had the best chance for breakout success. Simply clocking in at a corporate job will often get you enough money. You'll get a regular paycheck, solid benefits, and a reasonable amount of job security. But it won't get you to a meaningful leadership position. For that you need to be savvy, as Terry was, about where you can be a standout. Xerox would have been fine in the short term. Perhaps even in the long term. But Terry had a gut feeling about Bullocks, and he was right.

57

And, by the way, Terry did have to put off getting the new car he really wanted. But working at Bullock's, he was soon able to buy a late-model Ford Granada. While he says the Granada was very basic, the engine worked well.

GO WHERE THE MONEY IS

While the most lucrative corporate jobs are usually at the top, and getting one isn't a realistic goal as you're starting your career, it's a good idea to figure out which areas of the company are the most lucrative.

In virtually all cases, that means the place where revenue is created. Sales jobs almost always pay more than, say, production or human resources jobs. And if you're in an area that brings in money, and you're good at your job, you'll have a lot more security should the company have cutbacks. And if you *are* cut, you'll have more value in the job market.

Taking a corporate job when you're young can be a smart financial decision, in part because of the benefits. In fact, according to the Bureau of Labor Statistics, 32 percent of the average salary is in benefits. So it's worth taking the time to learn what you can get.

For example, when I had my first job at CNBC right out of college, the company would pay for me to take courses. I took advantage of the perk and got my Certificate in Financial Planning from New York University – completely free. Many companies will pay for their employees to get graduate degrees at nights or on weekends. Think about it: no student debt. And speaking of that, if you do graduate with debt look for companies that have policies that will pay some of your debt for you. This is often true at banking firms and consulting firms.

Companies will also often pay for memberships at networking organizations, which can be great resources as well. I was able to get my employer, Thomson Reuters, to pay for my membership to Ellevate, headed by Role Model Sallie Krawcheck, simply by asking my manager.

THE MOMMY (OR DADDY) TRACK

If you think you might want to take a break down the road, say for maternity leave, make sure you do a little research on that as well, and keep it in mind when you're choosing a company to join. It may seem like an obvious thing to research, but many young people take jobs with companies that are not family-friendly at all, and then they're shocked when they can't make it work.

Some may say that you should go for the most lucrative job and worry about family-friendliness later. But for many women (and men), a career they can continue without interruption, even at a lower compensation level, will end up being more lucrative than a career interrupted. Leaving the workforce for years is not a good financial move.

This isn't to say that you can't have priorities other than financial ones. Staying at home may be the right choice for you and your family. Having a parent at home full time can be priceless. But this is a book about the right financial decisions. So, in this context, any job that can offer career continuity will be a good financial choice.

I found two general scenarios of moms (or dads), who wanted to work, not going back to work after having kids:

Their childcare costs were too high relative to the salary they made.

Their job was so demanding that they literally would never see their children, and they would be paying someone else to raise them.

In both cases the men and women would express regret, at some level, that they hadn't chosen a company or career path that would have allowed them to continue working while raising a family, or pay them enough to be able to afford the support needed to be a working parent.

There are lots of lists out there on companies that are the most family-friendly. While we would all like to change the world, it's a lot easier to join a company that already makes a big, public push to be family-friendly than to try to convince a firm that doesn't make it a priority to change their culture and values.

The good news is that there is now a huge wave of corporations changing their family support policies. Netflix, for example, offers a full year of paid leave for parents. It doesn't have to be a solid year, so there is flexibility. A parent may want to come back for a few months for a special project and then return to their parental leave. Creative policies like this are generating new conversations about options, and many other companies are improving their policies.

According to *Working Mother* executive editor Jen Owens, companies have come a long way in the last 30 years since they've started keeping track of who does it best. There is more paid family leave, more childcare options, more scheduling flexibility, and more focus on women's advancement. She says that hundreds of companies compete to land a spot on the magazine's coveted list of most family-friendly companies. And as the job market tightens, things are likely to improve even more.

THE SIDE HUSTLE

I am a big fan of the side hustle. It's basically an extra job on top of your primary job, but with a real purpose. In some cases that purpose may be as simple as making more money to pay down debt.

My makeup artist Tonia Ciccone frequently works weddings and movies to make extra cash. She used that money to pay down a ton of credit card debt, boost her credit score, and build enough of a nest egg to buy a fantastic first home. She and her husband Joe are happily ensconced in a lovely home, in a great family neighborhood, and have a beautiful baby girl, Siena.

Tonia also made sure that her husband got a new, secure job with union benefits, including fantastic health insurance, before they had the baby. She is always thinking ahead, and it has really paid off.

Sometimes the side gig can be a way to pivot or enhance your career. You might have an idea for a product to sell. You can do that in your spare time and sell it on Etsy. Or if you're ready to write your novel, you can self-publish it. And for entrepreneurs, often the best companies are started as side projects while the founders continue the nine-to-five grind. If you have the time and energy, it's a great option.

YOUR FINANCIAL GROWNUP CHECKLIST
⁓ CAREERS ⁓

- ✓ Fake it 'til you make it.
- ✓ Follow up and say thank you to everyone.
- ✓ Make sure a career has earning potential – it's not a hobby.
- ✓ Know where in a company the money is made.
- ✓ Pay attention to benefits and company values.
- ✓ Think ahead to family priorities.
- ✓ Always have a side hustle.

CHAPTER FOUR

HOW TO SPEND MONEY

S PENDING MONEY IS EASY. Spending money on the right things at the right price, however, can require quite a bit of know-how. One way to have more money is to never spend it. We've all heard stories of little old ladies everyone thought were poor who passed away, only to leave millions to their heirs. Or young families who never left their homes, existed on homegrown food, and paid off their mortgages in just a few years. If that worked for them, great. But as anyone who has tried to diet by not eating can tell you, it makes a lot more sense to learn what to eat and in what portions. The challenge is drilling down to what matters, and figuring out how much it's worth to you. As you will see, happiness is usually not about accumulating more stuff.

This chapter will guide you on how to spend. Always make sure that the price is right for you. But if you pay attention to the other chapters in this book, you should have the financial resources to be able to spend on what matters most to achieve your dreams.

AMANDA STEINBERG

• FOUNDER, DAILYWORTH

MY FINANCIAL GROWNUP MOMENT

I had my headshots taken and I showed up on the cover of *Inc.* magazine's website, painting me as a success. I realized I was wearing clothes that were over five years old, and I looked really backwater. I looked like a hippie! I've always been kind of flower-childish, which is totally out of place in the finance world. This is business and this is how I'm perceived. When I saw those headshots I was embarrassed. I realized that I needed to pay more attention to my image.

MY LESSON TO SHARE

Image matters and you need to pay attention. I recently did a photoshoot for Marc Fisher shoes. I had my hair and makeup professionally done and the reaction I got was incredible. So many people said I looked amazing.

I often don't pay enough attention to how I am perceived. I do still cut corners – in fact I literally cut and dye my own hair! I'm a single mom. And I still carry the same bohemian handbag I've had for a decade. I'm still learning. I would say I'm 75 percent there.

FIGURE OUT WHAT MATTERS

DRESS FOR SUCCESS

EVERY TIME YOU consider spending on something, take a step back and ask yourself how that purchase will improve your life. Having yet another sweater probably won't improve your life. But in Amanda's case, having better headshots and a better magazine cover would improve her image, *Image* which could in turn help her business. Possible in- *matters* vestors or readers could see it and become more interested in her projects. Potential employees might have a better perception of the company and want to work there, allowing her to attract better employees. A stronger business would give her more financial resources and help her support her family, and thus improve her life.

Don't Penny Pinch on Principle

We talk so much about saving money and being frugal. But there's such a thing as cutting corners in the wrong places. It may seem frivolous to spend money on fancy clothing, or getting your makeup and hair done. Even if you aren't being photographed for a magazine, as Amanda was, your image matters in everything you do these days. To be clear, that doesn't mean that you should spend money indiscriminately on getting your hair done every day. But it's not a waste of money to do something to help you look your best on the day you're getting photos taken, as in Amanda's case.

These days the first impression you make is often on social media. Employers, potential clients, even people you meet networking are going to check out your LinkedIn page. Make sure your picture is good. More and more jobs expect you to have an active Twitter presence. Those images matter.

Playing Dress Up Isn't Just for Kids

Invest in clothes that are right both for the job you have and the job you want. Keep yourself up-to-date in how you present yourself at all times – you never know when you're going to run into someone. No one can be "on" at all times, but you should give yourself permission to spend the right amount of money to make sure you look your best.

That means dress like an adult at all times. You might just be running errands, but you may run into a friend who is with one of his or her friends who could be a great business contact. You may not look as polished as you would have liked, but it's real life, and that's not expected. But there's a big difference between neat and casual, and sloppy. Go for neat and casual – people will take you more seriously and value you more.

Fit Your Budget, and Yourself

Believe it or not, the most expensive clothing isn't always the best, even if it's in your budget. I have friends who have no budget, who spend a lot of money on clothing, and who often don't look all that great. I also have friends who are on a tight budget who somehow always look very put together.

The most important thing is that your clothes fit you well. Spend money on good tailoring. I can't tell you how many times I've bought a dress for a rock-bottom price on sale and spent more on tailoring than I did to buy the dress. But then I had a perfectly fitting garment that garnered a ton of compliments. The confidence that brings is worth it.

Why Buy When You Can Rent

There's a whole industry now devoted to renting outfits for special occasions. When you do need to splurge, this can be a great option. But always do the math.

If you have one big dressy event coming up on your calendar, and perhaps you're still losing baby weight (or, for the guys, baby sympathy weight) and expect to change sizes, renting is absolutely the way to go. Or if you're going to a theme party and you have to wear something that will just sit in your closet afterward, by all means, go for it.

But let's say you have five upcoming events that require dressing up. You may want to wear something different each time. But renting can add up if you aren't careful. We all see tons of images on Instagram of celebrities dressed up in glamorous outfits at awards shows. But you're not going to the Oscars (probably). You're probably going to your friend's wedding. Renting that $5,000 gown may "only" run you a few hundred dollars, but then you have nothing to show for your money, which you'll spend over and over to be seen in that $5,000 gown. And, as you're probably well aware, celebrities not only don't pay for the dresses and accessories they sport at awards shows, they usually don't even get to keep them! Talk about Cinderella syndrome.

Be a Repeat Offender

The reality is that you're probably better off investing in a $500 dress you can own. Princess Kate has won accolades wearing the same dress over and over. Her frugality has been celebrated. If you look and feel good in something, by all means, repeat. That blue dress you see on the cover of this book? I get a lot of compliments on it. So I wear it a lot. Come see me speak, and I just may be wearing it!

BEAUTY IS IN THE EYE OF THE CONSUMER

I knew I had finally made it in the television news business when I started having someone else do my hair and makeup. I also started to learn a lot about which products were worth spending more on and which ones were not – when the budget option was good enough. I used to think it was just about packaging. While that's a factor, there's more to the story.

So I reached out to *Shape* magazine Executive Beauty Editor Cheryl Kramer Kaye.

It's her job to try nearly every product available on the market, from the bargain-brand blushes to the most expensive eye cream. And nearly everyone who sees her personal bathroom stash has the same reaction: "You use drugstore products?"

Cheryl is a huge fan of mass brands. Those are often the companies that spend money on research and development rather than packaging and prestige. Of course she loves a little luxury, and there are certainly expensive products that are worth every penny. Keep in mind that these are generalizations, but here's where Cheryl says it's worth it to splurge, and where you can save big bucks.

Sunscreen: Save

This is by far the most important product in your skincare routine, since sun damage is about 80 percent of what we see as aging. Cheryl says that the key is finding one with proper UVA coverage, which means it contains either zinc oxide, titanium dioxide, or avobenzone, all of which are available in mass brands. Plus you want to apply your sunscreen generously, which you're less likely to do if it's costing you $10 an ounce.

Antioxidants: Splurge

Here's where packaging really does matter. Many free-radical fighters are sensitive to light and air and require special packaging that prevents them from degrading. But that packaging costs manufacturers more, so you're more likely to find them in higher-end stores and at dermatologists' offices.

Mascara: Save

Cheryl says almost all the cool innovations in mascara come from the drugstore brands, and the formulas are as good as if not better than the fancy stuff. Plus she advises everyone to toss out mascara every one to three months because of potential bacterial buildup, so don't waste your money on an expensive one.

Lipstick and Eyeshadow: Splurge

While you can certainly find something suitable at the drugstore, the best shade ranges – and the ability to try before you buy – make the department store the best bet for trend-driven items such as lipstick and eyeshadow. And is there anything more glamorous than pulling out a tube or compact of Chanel/Armani/Tom Ford from your purse? Cheryl is also a big fan of the free gift with purchase: nothing makes her heart swell like a freebie to sample. (*Insider tip from Cheryl: Many department store counters have samples stashed away, even if they're not running a promotion – just ask!*)

Fragrance: Splurge

You know why Journey sang, "a smell of wine and cheap perfume?" Because everyone knows what cheap perfume smells like – strong, sweet, and headache-inducing. By and large there are more natural ingredients in high-end fragrance and more synthetic ingredients in inexpensive ones. And your nose can tell the difference.

Hair Products: No Verdict

Cheryl says she would go to the ends of the earth and spend any amount of money on the various products in the conditioner-shampoo-styling cocktail that works for her. Some of the bottles are super-cheap and others are pretty pricey. This is one case where it's not about the cost of the products. Cheryl says you just have to keep trying until you find the combination that makes your own mane manageable.

THE LATTE THING

Ever since David Bach started advocating that we all cut out those lattes, there's been an incredible amount of talk about coffee as a discretionary expense. To be fair, in Bach's case he's using expensive coffee as a metaphor for life's repeated, every-day expenses that add up without you being aware of it. He's right – it's about paying attention to what you're spending.

But the coffee analogy has taken on a life of its own. Even Role Model Kevin O'Leary has insisted to me that no one should ever purchase expensive coffee drinks. He told me he even forbids his employees to do so! The truth is that to a large degree they're right – coffee drinks are often an overpriced indulgence.

That said, as someone who regularly treats herself to coffee drinks I do feel compelled to add a couple of exceptions to "never."

- Buy coffee at a coffee shop if you're going there for social reasons. Meeting friends at a coffee shop is going to be a lot cheaper than going out for a meal.

- If you're using the coffee shop as an ad hoc office, by all means buy some coffee. Sitting at a coffee shop for a few hours to get some work done, or to have a meeting, is a lot less expensive than paying rent on an office.

It also matters what you buy – the fancy espresso drinks will kill your wallet. Do the math and you'll immediately stop. When New York City started putting calorie counts on their pastries, I stopped eating one of my favorites – a 490-calorie lemon pound cake slice. Once you see the numbers behind your actions, you'll change. Just have a regular coffee or tea for a quarter of the price – it's less money and fewer calories.

Like David Bach, we're using *coffee* as a metaphor here, and you should apply the philosophy above to any mindless habits you spend money supporting. You may take taxis when you really don't need to. You may throw a lot of discretionary items in your cart at the supermarket. You may over-order at restaurants, even when you aren't that hungry. Whatever your mindless vice is, think about it, and make a deliberate decision to pay attention to how much you're paying to indulge in it.

THE PAYROLL

Many of us don't realize it, but we spend a lot on what I call the payroll. Some expenses are unavoidable. If you have a child you probably have to pay for childcare. But there may be other "employees" you may want to think twice about. For example, having a maid or housekeeper is great and may be worth the money. But be careful about how often they come. If they currently come once a week, maybe have them come every other week, and do a little more yourself. Or, if you buy a house, learn to mow the lawn yourself. If you pay a dog walker, see if you can double up with a neighbor and have the dogs walked together for a discount. Outsourcing things you can do yourself can be expensive.

That said, there are times when outsourcing may make sense, such as having a housekeeper who can make dinner for your family if you have long work hours. That allows you to focus your time and mental energy on your career, creating value. You can then spend time doing homework with your child (possibly avoiding a tutor down the road), relax with your significant other, or just have some down time to clear your head instead of cleaning and making dinner in the precious few hours you do have off from work. You can't do it all. But you should be mindful of the cost and how you spend that part of your budget.

GIVING AND GETTING A DEAL

As anyone who has ever gone to a benefit knows, sometimes items, especially in a silent auction, go for less than their fair market value. What few people realize is that many organizations now run virtual auctions to raise money, and you don't have to have any affiliation with the school or charity to snag a deal.

For example, auction site Bidding for Good has a long list of auctions going at any given time. Many items go for below their retail price. Plus you're giving to a good cause.

FIND THE OPEN SECRETS

Many of the best things in life can be had for a fraction of their face value. You just need to do a little work to know how to get that lower price. Case in point: Broadway. Most shows have some sort of rush ticket, or lottery. The face value of tickets can be upwards of $200, but rush tickets can be had for as little as $20. Each show has different rules – all you have to do is go to their website. There's even an app, Todaytix.com, where you can get lower-cost Broadway tickets. It's just a case of knowing where to get the deal, and being ready when it's available.

Bricks and Mortar Tricks of the Trade

Similar open secrets exist across the spectrum of items and experiences. Dealing with a live human being can be a great way to get a deal. When you go to a store chat up the salesperson and ask if an item is going on sale in the next two weeks. At many department stores a sales person can look up when, say, a friends-and-family-sale is coming and can sell the items to you on pre-sale. You simply reserve the item and pick it up a few days later when the sale officially starts. If you don't have time to go back, they will mail it to you. Ask (nicely) for free shipping.

And don't forget the ubiquitous price match. Anytime you buy something that's sold somewhere else, take the time to search on your phone for a cheaper price, and then ask for a price match. Sometimes the store will even give you 10 percent below the competition. But they won't offer unless you ask, nicely.

Get the Code

Here's another open secret: Take the time to search the Internet for discount codes. Everyone knows this, but we often forget or we're lazy and just want to get on with our purchase. I bought furniture online, and at the last minute I found 40-percent-off coupon codes, slashing the price I paid. Retailmenot.com and Coupon.com are popular places to find discount codes. There's also a browser extension called Honey that basically automates applying coupon codes to your cart. This also works if you're in a store. Take out your cellphone, search for a coupon code or a deal using an app like Shopsavvy or Pricegrabber, and have the salesperson apply it. If for some reason they won't, buy it online on your phone right there in front of them. Don't leave money on the table – make the effort.

Take a Time Out

I discovered this by accident, and then asked around and found I wasn't alone. I was shopping for a jacket, put it in my online cart, and had to go run an errand. When I came back a few hours later and opened my computer, there was a pop-up window with a code for 10 percent off if I completed the order! I would have bought the jacket anyway, so the discount was a nice extra. But many stores will send you an additional discount to seal the deal. Abandoned carts are a big issue for them. So, if you have the time, fill your basket, and then take a time out. When you come back the retailer may have sweetened the deal.

Be a Friend

Becoming friends with your favorite brands is a great way to hear about discounts. Follow them on social media and you'll be rewarded. The caveat: It's a two-way street. They have your info and will also market to you. Try out your favorites, and if their marketing is too aggressive decide whether the discounts are worth it. One way to make it work: set up a separate email account just for these kinds of lists. That way your shopping is compartmentalized, and you have more control. You can also use sites such as trackif. com to get notified if prices come down on things you have on your wish list. A popular price tracker is CamelCamelCamel. Be informed, and make the decision that's right for you.

THE BIG-TICKET ITEM

Sometimes we hesitate to make a big purchase that drains our bank account. And if you get that sinking feeling in your stomach, you should think carefully about that big splurge. Take a step back if it's an unnecessary indulgence. But trust your instinct to know whether something will help you achieve your goals, as was the case with our next Role Model.

ADAM NASH

• CEO, WEALTHFRONT

MY FINANCIAL GROWNUP MOMENT

In October 1993 I spent over $3,000 on an Apple Quadra 800.

I know that seems like a lot of money for a computer that lacks the appeal of a new MacBook Air, but in fairness, it was a high-end model for the time, with 24 megabytes of RAM and a 500-megabyte hard drive.

I was just starting my junior year at Stanford and had completed my first internship as a software engineer at Hewlett-Packard in Palo Alto. It was the most money I had ever made. I had been paid $2,235 per month for 10 weeks, and that computer cost me a significant portion of my entire summer's earnings. But it was the best money I've ever spent.

Invest in your skills

Like many students I had declared my major during my sophomore year and had chosen computer science. I was fortunate enough to have my own computer, a Macintosh LC, that my parents had been generous enough to provide for me when

I arrived at college. But as I pushed deeper into the field, I found myself facing long compile times and memory limitations with my computer, a machine that really wasn't optimized for software development.

In many ways that purchase represented the beginning of my financial independence. I had declared a major in a field of study that had led directly to the best job I had ever had. I then decided to personally reinvest the earnings into equipment that I believed would further my development.

More importantly, rather than placing a further burden on my parents, it was my first significant independent purchase.

MY LESSON TO SHARE

It's hard to quantify the value of investing in your own skills, and then having them rewarded with financial independence.

Looking back now over 20 years in the software industry, it's hard not to be nostalgic for that Quadra 800 – the first computer I ever purchased.

SPEND WHEN IT MATTERS

THE LINE THAT stands out here is that Nash reinvested his earnings into equipment that he believed would further his development. His confidence in the bold decision to make that purchase is not that different from Amanda Steinberg's regret at not investing in what turned out to be important to her.

Adam spent money investing in something that mattered and would make him more successful. Buying it with his own money increased its value all the more. Now that's a grownup moment.

TECHNOLOGY: COMING IN FIRST ISN'T WINNING

These days upgrade cycles are getting shorter and shorter, so it's tricky to figure out the optimal time to swap out technology. There's no magic answer. Like Adam, the secret is in paying attention to your actual needs. Most of us don't need a new smartphone every six months, or even every two years. In the United States, carriers for years set up systems that hooked us into two-year commitments, which made us think that that was the optimal time to get a new phone. That system is being disrupted by innovative new pricing plans that open up contracts but have users paying more directly for their devices. It gives us more reason to think about whether that upgrade makes sense.

The same is true for other devices, whether it be tablets, laptops, or PCs. Think about what you do with your technology. If you're just emailing and using basic apps, stick with what you've got. But if, for example, you're a graphic designer who needs to always have the top technology and the devices to support it, then make the changes you need to optimize your business.

CASH IN THE OLD TO BRING IN THE NEW

If you do decide it's time to get new stuff, make sure to cash out your used devices. Websites such as Gazelle.com and uSell will take your electronics and send you cash. By the way, some websites, such as uSell, also buy other items, including textbooks and gift cards.

Many retailers will buy your old stuff. The catch is that payment is often in the form of credit, which they hope you'll use (and add to) to buy even better stuff from them. And in many cases you will, so this can be a great deal for you.

Perhaps the most important lesson here is that you can't go on a spending starvation diet. You have to allow yourself to spend. But as Role Model Jill Kargman points out, that doesn't mean you can skip doing the math.

JILL KARGMAN

- BESTSELLING AUTHOR
- STAR OF *ODD MOM OUT*

MY FINANCIAL GROWNUP MOMENT

I started getting an allowance of about two bucks a week. I would save it for snacks, after school, and by 5th grade it was $5 a week. And I would save it up, and I would take the cross-town bus and go to Tower Records and spend it on vinyl records, and you know I feel like I just knew what was on sale, and I would follow the albums, and if the album was new how expensive it was. I just was always saving. I always added things up and did the math on it all.

> *Sock away as much as you can*

MY LESSON TO SHARE

Sock away as much as you can. I think experiential things are important, and I know a lot of people are spending every dollar they make to go to fun bars or restaurants, and that's all important, but you have to save, too.

YOUR FINANCIAL GROWNUP CHECKLIST
∼ SPENDING ∼

- Grownups know how to spend money.
- Don't pinch pennies when it comes to your image.
- Ask for free samples.
- Avoiding spending on the right things will cost you.
- Know when it pays to rent vs. own things such as clothing.
- Be strategic and patient to get the best price.
- Shop non-traditionally, including charity auctions.
- Get social to score better deals from favorite retailers.
- Cash in what you have to help finance upgrades.
- Spend on tools that will make you more productive.
- Do the math.

CHAPTER FIVE

INVESTING STARTS NOW

My grandpa Harry used to sing all the time. One day I asked him why he was singing. He said he was happy the stock market was down. I was surprised because that sounded like a bad thing. But he told me it was a good thing, because now he could buy the stocks he wanted at a better price. The next day he was singing again. Only this time he said he was singing because the market went up. He explained that the stocks he owned were worth more.

Don't get caught up waiting on the sidelines for the perfect investment and the perfect price. Be smart, of course – research investments carefully. But get started today. I remember interviewing Role Model Kevin O'Leary on a day stocks were getting crushed. The Dow was down 500 points. Kevin was buying. He even told me, and my viewers, exactly what he was buying. You'll never make money sitting on the sidelines. Get in the game.

ROGER CRANDALL

- CHAIRMAN, PRESIDENT, AND CEO, MASSACHUSETTS MUTUAL LIFE INSURANCE COMPANY (MASSMUTUAL)

MY FINANCIAL GROWNUP MOMENT

My financial grownup moment came when I was in high school and I started to learn about investing from none other than Albert Einstein, who is often quoted as saying, "Compound interest is the eighth wonder of the world. He who understands it, earns it . . . he who doesn't . . . pays it."

It came up recently during a conversation with my son, Thomas. He just turned 19 and I convinced him to start putting money into an IRA. When I asked him how long he planned on working, he shrugged and said, "I don't know – 75 or 80?" He was right – with Americans living longer, working longer, and our social safety net continuing to shrink, this younger generation is likely to work longer than we or our parents ever did.

I gave him some examples – at just a five percent interest rate, your money can grow 30 times over 70 years, and by more than 130 times over 100 years. Einstein was wise enough to know there's as much – if not more – power in a calculator than in the cosmos.

MY LESSON TO SHARE

Two words: start early. We all need to take greater control of our own financial future at a time when we're living longer. For many, pensions have been largely replaced by 401(k) plans that require us to contribute from each paycheck. We have a social safety net that may not be much of a net in the future, given where we're headed. And by 2050 we're expected to have 84 million people in the U.S. over the age of 65, nearly double what we have today. All of this points to the need for us to start saving as early as we can. It doesn't matter if it's a lot – as long as it's something . . . *anything.*

Also, an added benefit of starting early: this leads to good money habits for the rest of your life. As you grow up, life grows complicated, and that's especially the case with money. Whether it's buying a house, raising a family, starting a business, or caring for elderly parents, all of these events revolve around finances. And they'll be some of the biggest decisions you'll ever make. Saving early helps you recognize the value of a dollar at an early age and, ultimately, leads you on the right path to making smarter decisions down the road.

START INVESTING EARLY

CRANDALL IS right. We're all living and working longer. So we have the power of compounding in our favor. We also have more urgency to get started earlier, because our money has to last that much longer.

I asked Roger to be a role model for this project specifically because the company he leads, MassMutual, recognized the need to get people interested in paying more attention to their finances.

Saving early helps you recognize the value of a dollar

The company started the Society for Grownups, which provides accessible and realistic financial advice for emerging adults. They offer classes, chats, supper clubs, networking events, and even individual sessions with Certified Financial Planners. The goal: make it easy to get started, so that people actually get started.

Sometimes the hardest thing to admit and embrace is that you're a grownup, and that you need to proactively pay attention to your finances and investments. Crandall's son Thomas, at age 19, may not be sure how long he's going to work, but he can't go wrong by starting an IRA when he's still a teen.

For most of us, our financial grownup moment happens when we're in our 20s or 30s and forming a family and getting into the heart of a career. But the process is often gradual, and sometimes we're even past those years and well into middle age when the financial grownup moment hits. I'm not going to lie – younger is better. But any age is better than never.

For those who don't feel they need one-on-one, in-person advice, or simply can't afford it, one of the biggest recent trends has been the emergence of so-called robo-advisors.

Companies such as Wealthfront, headed by Role Model Adam Nash, and Betterment, led by Role Model Jon Stein, are reaching out to investors with this innovative approach to investing and financial planning. Established companies such as Schwab, Vanguard, and Fidelity have been entering this growing field. Some of these companies have no account minimums and fees are often a fraction of those of a traditional money manager or brokerage. Most importantly, they excel in automation and efficiency. In other words, they will pay attention to your investment choices for you, after that initial decision to sign up. There is no excuse to not start.

BASIC THINGS TO THINK ABOUT WHEN IT COMES TO INVESTING

Don't jump the gun: You should always keep enough cash on hand to get you through any immediate cash needs.

Generally that means enough to cover six to nine months of living expenses in case something unexpected happens. Also put aside money you'll need in the next couple of years for any big expenses, such as a mortgage. Those can go into basic savings accounts, money market accounts, or Certificates of Deposit (CDs), though none of those will pay you much. Your money will, however, be there when you need it.

PLANNING FOR RETIREMENT

You may be young, but we can't repeat Roger Crandall's advice enough: the compounding power of investing at a young age is the most powerful tool you have.

Certified Financial Planner Cary Carbonaro, Managing Director of United Capital and author of *The Money Queen's Guide,* illustrates Roger's point that small amounts of money turn into large ones over time thanks to compounding. Her example: if you saved $200 a month or $2,400 a year beginning at age 21, using an 8 percent return, at age 65 you would have $856,679.

The most important thing is that you get in the game. And if you're older, don't waste time looking back. Just move on, and get started immediately.

401(k)s

A 401(k) is a retirement savings account offered by companies. The money goes in pre-tax, so it will lower your tax bill. The 401(k) holds investments in it, like a basket – you choose which mutual funds to allocate your money to from a pre-selected list of invest-ment options.

This is often the best place to save for retirement, especially *if your company offers a match.* If your company does offer one, invest at least the amount they match from day one. Many com-panies match dollar for dollar up to six percent. Most plans have a box you can check that allows you to automatically up your savings percentage by a certain amount each year. Click at least one per-cent. You can always change it. But you probably won't. And that's a good thing.

401(k) Fees

There's one big red flag with 401(k)s: fees. Many have very high costs for employees. If your employer matches your contributions, that will in most cases offset those fees. But if not, you should do some math, and consider other options, which we'll discuss later. But CFP Cary Carbonaro warns, you have no choice or options with 401(k) fees – it's whatever your company offers. That said, it may be worth approaching your company's decision makers and making them aware of the high fees. It will take time, but a good employer will make changes to get a better deal for it's employees.

This is an issue Role Model Tony Robbins, who you will hear from later in the book, has been raising the red flag on. He has created a fee checker – http://americasbest401k.com/fee-checker/ – to help educate people on what they are paying. When I interviewed him about this topic, he told me that every 1 percent more in fees takes away 10 years of future retirement income. He also pointed out that, on average, 401(k) fees are a whopping 3.1 percent.

One little known fact: many mutual funds pay to be included in plans. Tony even compares it to the pay-to-play era when record labels paid to get their talent on the radio. He advises looking for index fund options within your company's plan, which often have the lowest fees.

Other Expenses to Look For

The biggest fee is often the expense ratio. You can find this in the prospectus for the mutual fund you choose within the 401(k). Morningstar is also a great resource. Since you choose the investments within the 401(k), this is one expense you'll likely have some control over.

According to Kyle Ramsay, Head of Investing & Retirement at NerdWallet, if the expense ratio is above 1 percent, you should carefully consider if that's the best option for you. A ratio below 0.5 percent is "good," below 0.25 percent is "very good."

Here's the math: if you're paying 1 percent extra in fees for 30 years (6 percent annual return), it can reduce your ultimate nest egg by 25 percent ! That means $123,000 on a $100,000 initial balance.

Also, Ramsey says to look out for plan operating expenses. Many employers will pay these for you, but some smaller companies can't afford to do that. You can find this number in your plan's summary annual report.

Finally, look out for trading commissions (or loads), 12b-1 fees, wrap fees, and other transaction expenses. In addition to eating away at your nest egg, these can affect the decision to rebalance your funds since you would incur a transaction cost each time. You can get all this information and more regarding mutual funds and other investments at Morningstar.com, the investment research company created by Role Model Joe Mansueto.

A great place to see how your company's 401(k) stacks up is BrightScope.com. You can literally type in your employer's name, and it will show you how it ranks against others. BrightScope will also show you a breakdown of the fees.

One way to keep investment costs down in general is to contribute enough to your 401(k) to capture your employer's match for the year, then start contributing to an IRA or Roth IRA if you're eligible, which will offer wider access to low-cost investments. If you max out the IRA, start contributions to the 401(k) again.

Roth IRAs

These are for after-tax money. If you invest when you're young, your taxes are probably relatively low. And when money is taken out, there are no taxes on the original contribution, or the gains. Another feature – you can access the money. And if it's for a new home, or higher education, there are no financial penalties, although in some cases there may be income taxes due. There is a limit to how much you can contribute, and there are income limits (the amount you can contribute to a Roth IRA is determined by your income level).

Traditional IRAs

These go to your account pre-tax, so they can make your tax bill go down right away, just like a 401(k). However, there's a catch: If your employer provides a retirement savings account, such as a 401(k), you may not be eligible for the tax deduction. There are also income limitations. While you can access the money at any time, if you take it out before age 59½ you'll pay a 10 percent penalty, and you'll also pay the income tax you avoided on the way in.

INVESTING FOR LIFE

Once you've got your retirement savings set on automatic pilot, it makes sense to start investing any extra cash you may have.

Individual Stocks

Investing in individual stocks is not for the faint of heart, and it's generally not a good idea if you don't have a ton of cash you can afford to lose. Unless you have enough investable assets to basically create your own mutual fund, you won't be diversified and will be vulnerable to any bit of bad news that hits a stock. Those stories about the taxi driver making big sums betting on one stock? Not likely these days. Unless you have the time, money, and stomach to lose your shirt, leave it to the pros.

Index Funds

This is a great option for many investors. Index funds are mutual funds or ETFs that track an index like a stock. You won't ever beat the market – but who cares? Historically the market has always headed higher, and if history repeats itself so will your investments. More importantly, as Tony Robbins advises, you won't be paying lots of commissions and fees. Index funds are almost universally great deals for investors.

Mutual Funds

These pool together investors' money to buy a basket of individual securities, which could be stocks, bonds, futures, etc. Most will have a set mission. For example, one might focus on stocks that invest in socially responsible companies. Or they might invest in a certain type of debt. The key here is to look not only at how the fund has performed (which can change dramatically anyway) but also at the fees and expenses. Some funds even charge fees to buy and sell. High fees will eat up your returns, and with the resources available today, that's just wrong. Also beware the tax man. If the fund sells stocks, you may get hit with capital gains taxes. You also may receive dividends into your account and get a tax hit for that as well.

Exchange Traded Funds (ETFs)

In some ways these are similar to mutual funds in that you're getting a basket of securities. Also, like mutual funds, they often have a core investing strategy. For example, Role Model Kevin O'Leary's O'Shares focuses on his belief that the best stocks to invest in are those that pay dividends.

Unlike mutual funds, ETFs trade like stocks. That means you can sell in the middle of the trading day if you want. With mutual funds you have to wait until the close of business. Also, they tend to be lower cost and more tax efficient than many mutual funds, especially when they follow an index. Finally, you can buy just one share of an ETF, which makes for a lower barrier to entry.

529 Plans

These are college savings plans, most likely for your kids or, if you're a grandparent, for your grandkids. The money grows tax-deferred, and in some states may be eligible for state income tax deductions. The money can be used for education-related expenses, including books and tuition, at colleges, universities, and vocational schools.

TAXES AND INVESTING

As you can see from the options above, while top-line returns are important in investing, both fees and taxes can make a huge difference as well. Many of the robo-advisors automatically take taxes into consideration when making investment moves.

Here's a basic explainer from CFP Cary Carbonaro:

Tax-Deferred Accounts

If you're investing in a tax-deferred account such as a 401(k), 457(b), 403(b), Roth IRA, or traditional IRA, taxes will have no impact on your investing until you take money out. The entire time you're investing that money is tax deferred. To be clear, that means the only time you pay taxes is when you take money out.

Once you reach 59½ there are no penalties. If you take money out before then you'll get a 10 percent tax penalty, and it will be added to your income.

If the money is in a Roth IRA, the account has to have been open for five years for all the principal and earnings to be tax free based on the current tax laws.

Taxable or Non-qualified Money

Carbonaro also offers ideas for tax-managing your investments that don't fit into the kinds of accounts described above.

Qualified Dividends

You can invest in stocks or ETFs that have Qualified Dividends. Since 2003 these dividends have been subject to the same tax rates as long-term capital gains, which are lower than rates for ordinary income.

Municipal Bonds

You can invest in municipal bonds, bond funds, or ETFs. You have to calculate your taxable equivalent yield (TEY) to decide if a tax-free investment is worth it. If you have a bond paying 2.5 percent taxable and a municipal bond paying 1.9 percent not taxable, you need to know which is better for you. Here's the way it works: If you are in a 55-percent tax bracket for city, state, and federal taxes, you take 1 minus your tax bracket – in this case, 1 minus .55, which equals .45. Then you take 1.9 divided by .45, which makes a taxable equivalent yield of 4.2 percent. This is why it usually makes sense for high wage earners to invest in municipal bonds.

TAXES AND TIME (SHORT-TERM AND LONG-TERM GAINS AND LOSSES)

Short-term Capital Gains

Short-term capital gains do not benefit from any special tax rate, says Carbonaro. They're taxed at the same rate as your ordinary income. For 2015 ordinary tax rates ranged from 10 percent to 39.6 percent, depending on your total taxable income.

If you sell an asset you've held for one year or less, any profit you make is considered a short-term capital gain. The clock begins ticking from the day after you acquire the asset up to and including the day you sell it.

Long-term Capital Gains

There are advantages to holding investments for longer than a year. You can often benefit from a reduced tax rate on your profits. For 2015 the long-term capital gains tax rates for federal taxes were 0, 15, and 20 percent, depending on your tax bracket. If your ordinary tax rate is already less than 15 percent, you could qualify for the zero-percent, long-term capital gains rate!

Tax Loss Harvesting

A potential benefit of taxable accounts is the ability to use your losses to pay less money on the money you made with your profitable investments.

Carbonaro explains what happens when you sell a security that you've lost money on. By realizing, or harvesting, a loss, investors are able to offset capital gains taxes on both gains and income. This is usually done at year end. You can get rid of what's down and book a tax loss on your taxes for that year. If you don't have any gains to offset, you can carry forward your unused losses, up to $3,000 a year.

Don't Get Carried Away

It's important not to let the tax tail wag the dog. Don't make investment decisions because of taxes. But always figure out the tax implications of the decisions you make, and factor them in. That may mean selling an asset at the end of a calendar year if you're going to take a loss, which can offset other gains. Or waiting a day or so into the new year to sell an asset with a big gain so you can push that gain into the next tax year. Many of the robo-advisors have features built in to help with these decisions. It may also be worth it, if you have unique circumstances or have doubts, to do a consultation with a fee-only CFP or other professional.

RETIREMENT: PROCRASTINATING WILL COST YOU

According to PwC, only 36 percent of young people ages 23 to 34 even have a retirement account. And of those, 17 percent borrowed from that account. That's downright financially immature.

When you're young, you have something truly magical on your side, which is time, says Manisha Thakor, Director of Wealth Strategies for Women at Buckingham and The BAM ALLIANCE. She advises committing right out of the gate to saving 10 percent of your income each and every year for retirement. Invest those hard-earned dollars in low-cost index or target-date retirement funds, and let time work its magic. Thanks to the magic of compounding, if you save $5,000 a year from age 25 to age 70, and earn 6 percent on your investments, you'll have a million-dollar retirement nest egg.

The math is pretty dramatic, according to Thakor. If you wait until you're in your mid-40s to start saving, you would need to up that annual savings figure to a whopping $25,000 to end up with the same size nest egg.

The bottom line: Each dollar you save for the future in your 20s is nearly five times as valuable as one you save later on.

Thakor says to think of it like sunscreen. If you use it regularly in your 20s and 30s, you may not look that different from your peers. But as the years progress it becomes increasingly obvious who did, and who did not, use sunscreen – and the corrective steps you have to take at a later stage in life can be expensive and painful.

STEPHEN ADLER

- PRESIDENT AND EDITOR-IN CHIEF, REUTERS

MY FINANCIAL GROWNUP MOMENT

In the mid-'80s, many bank CDs were paying interest of 12 percent or more, and banks were tripping over each other to offer the highest rates to entice small-timers like me who contributed each year to Individual Retirement Accounts (IRAs). The difference between banks was often in the quarter of a percent range, but it was nonetheless clear to me – as a young adult seeking to be financially savvy – that I urgently needed to eke out the best possible deal for my $2,000 IRA.

So, in the pre-Internet age, I checked newspaper ads and raced around from bank to bank on my lunch break to compare rates and consider where to put that precious money. One day I saw an ad for a CD at a bank in the Bronx and got set to head up there. My boss, *American Lawyer Magazine* editor-in-chief and budding mogul Steven Brill, asked where I was going – and put an abrupt stop to my journey. He sat me down in his office and showed me on a yellow legal pad how much my time was worth at my job versus how much I would earn by leaving my desk to score an extra quarter point on a bank CD. And, in stronger language than I'm using here, he told me what a jerk I was for not understanding that my biggest asset and investment at this life stage was my job – not my IRA – and that the energy I was putting into chasing CD alpha was better spent writing and editing for his magazine.

MY LESSON TO SHARE

He was right on one particular – that one needs as a young person to internalize the concept of "penny-wise, pound-foolish," and that I certainly hadn't done so. And he was really right on the larger point, that one's salary and income potential are huge components of any investment plan. And that's what I'd advise any young adult today: Getting and holding a job, and doing the kind of work that might lead to getting promoted, are a whole lot more important than picking the right stock or the hottest fund or the perfect CD.

DON'T GET LOST IN THE WEEDS

WHAT ADLER MAKES clear is this – don't get lost in the weeds of investing. Invest the money you can. But don't obsess. Spending all day watching financial news and researching individual stocks should not take the place of focusing on your career and your life. Keep it in perspective.

The good news is that there are a lot of ways to get your money invested in a thoughtful, efficient, and responsible way, and then move on.

JOE MANSUETO

• CEO, MORNINGSTAR, INC.

MY FINANCIAL GROWNUP MOMENT

I was into ham radio when I was in grade school. We'd build short-wave receivers and transmitters and talk to people all over the world. I thought it was pretty cool. One day I was at a ham fest, where people bought and sold radio equipment. I went with my friend and his parents.

I came across a guy who was getting out of ham radio and selling his equipment. He had a Drake 2-B receiver that I knew was worth at least $150 and probably much more. He was selling it for $80. So I borrowed the funds from my friends' parents and bought it. It was the biggest purchase I had ever made, but I was confident there was value.

I then took out an ad in a ham radio publication and sold it for $160. I made an $80 profit, which seemed like an incredible sum to me. It was the first time I made a profit from something other than chores, and it opened my eyes to business and investing.

MY LESSON TO SHARE

The lesson I learned was the importance of understanding value. The only reason I made a profit on the ham radio sale was because I was confident in my value assessment, even after allowing for a good margin of safety. Most people develop this ability in areas they are active in – food shoppers, for example, know when bananas are selling at attractive price. As you expand your domain expertise (ham radio in my case), you can use these same skills to your advantage. If you want to buy stocks, you need that same ability to place a value on a company to know whether it's a good buy.

Conversely, if you don't know the intrinsic worth of something (like the seller of the Drake 2-B receiver), you can quickly erode your capital. So the deeper domain expertise you have, the better an investor you'll be.

Understand value –
the intrinsic worth of things

YOUR FINANCIAL GROWNUP CHECKLIST
∽ INVESTING ∽

- Get started young, or now, whichever is sooner.

- Get your cash emergency fund in order first.

- Robo-advisors make investing more accessible.

- Don't fall for fees you don't have to pay.

- Don't leave money on the table – grab the 401(k) match.

- Always factor in taxes.

- Don't get caught up in the minutia of an investment decision.

- Choose investments where you know the true value.

CHAPTER SIX

FAMILY MATTERS

ASK A FINANCIALLY SUCCESSFUL PERSON what drives them, and you'll often hear them talk about their family. Sometimes it's about making a parent proud, or about setting a good example for kids. It's almost always tied to being a provider for their spouse and children.

But family life and the emotional relationships that go with it also complicate our ability to make and manage money. Many marriages fall apart because of money issues. Divorce is a notoriously bad financial move. And the family demands of having children can often wreak havoc on even the most well-intentioned financial planning efforts.

Love and family bonds also can cloud our judgment. What parent hasn't gone over budget to get that big smile from a child desperate for a toy they can't afford? And when you marry the love of your life and promise to spend the rest of your lives together, who can blame you if you trust your significant other with the bank accounts . . . as was the case for a young Sallie Krawcheck.

SALLIE KRAWCHECK

• FOUNDER, ELLEVATE

MY FINANCIAL GROWNUP MOMENT

My financial grown-up moment happened when I was 28 years old. I had married young, to someone I was madly in love with. We were living the dream, living in London, living in New York, and building our careers. And then there were a couple little signs of something being amiss. Not big signs, just little ones. He left my sister's wedding early "for work"; when I returned the guest room curtains were tied back incorrectly, and there was a dark hair on the bedspread. So I made a note to myself to ask him if he was having an affair . . . and promptly forgot to, for several days.

When I remembered to ask him, he said no. I asked again; he said no. I turned away and felt a little jolt of electricity, and asked one more time. His response: "You're gonna be mad." He was right; I was pretty mad.

Not only was I mad, but I also felt stupid. Here I was, building a career on Wall Street, but managing my own finances like a 1950s-era, stay-at-home housewife. He paid the bills, he made the financial decisions. I didn't even know what our assets were.

I never expected my marriage to end, so the division of labor felt like it made sense. It didn't. It just didn't.

MY LESSON TO SHARE

Any number of years on, my advice is for all of us to be engaged in our finances. Stuff happens, stuff you don't expect. People get unexpectedly divorced, and people pass away unexpectedly. Combining the trauma of these things (I went down to 108 pounds during my divorce) with the confusion over getting up to speed on finances . . . with the spouse possibly out of the picture . . . is a recipe for financial disaster.

GETTING MARRIED? – BE PREPARED FOR THE UNEXPECTED

SALLIE KRAWCHECK IS known as one of the savviest women in the business world, having headed up a number of Wall Street firms. She is now the brains behind Ellevate, a huge global professional women's network, and recently launched an investment arm. She's also one of the most resilient, determined, and, dare I say, heroic women in business today. But she's the first to admit she wasn't financially savvy when it came to marriage – at least the first time around.

The good news is that young people are getting married later and have a better shot at making smarter financial decisions.

As more couples have two working partners, both are often more aware of the stake they have in the family finances.

MONEY: THE TABOO TOPIC

According to Fidelity, 43 percent of couples don't know what their partners earn. That's despite the fact that almost three quarters of them say they communicate well. The same study found that 36 percent of couples disagree about how much investable assets they have. So take a lesson from Krawcheck and have the talk now. Also decide together who will be in charge of the family finances, and keep the other one informed.

MARRIAGE AS FINANCIAL MERGER

Society puts a huge emphasis on marrying for love, at least in the United States. But the truth is, whom you marry is also the biggest financial decision of your life. You are literally betting your entire future on someone else. Their career success is tied to your support, and vice versa. The same goes for investment success.

That said, it's not about marrying *for* money, but marrying someone who has the same money goals and values. You may want to spend all your money traveling, while your love wants to invest in a big house. Or one of you wants a luxury lifestyle, even if it means being workaholics, while the other is happy to have a little less, if it means having more family time. You need to be on the same page and have the same expectations.

GET FINANCIALLY NAKED

Tell each other everything. Have a specific conversation. Don't assume your love would volunteer their financial dirty laundry. I've heard quite a few stories about post-wedding chats where the bride or groom discloses credit card debt or a terrible credit score. It happens. People lie by omission for fear you will judge them, or hold it against them. Sometimes people are just embarrassed.

Go over the assets each of you has, and where they are. This includes checking and savings accounts, investments, retirement funds, and cash under the mattress. Then go over the debts. This includes student debt, car loans, credit card balances, home equity loans, money you may have lent to friends or family, and so on. Finally talk about budgeting and financial priorities, and come to at least a broad framework of how you both want to allocate your resources as a family.

AGREE TO BE FINANCIALLY FAITHFUL AS PART OF YOUR PROMISE TO EACH OTHER

Money is often cited as the biggest cause of divorce. By merging your finances when you get hitched, you lose your financial freedom.

Emily and Evan got into big trouble with this. They had been married for a few years and had two young sons. They lived in a beautiful suburb near where both had grown up. Her husband's family business was not doing well. But he didn't want her to worry. She was a stay-at-home mom, who had grown up in a financially comfortable family. She had never really thought about having financial troubles. She spent money as she needed. She wasn't extravagant, but she had no reason to think she should be on any real budget.

Evan paid the bills, so Emily had no idea that they were falling behind. He didn't want her to worry, so he didn't say anything. He just hoped things would get better. They didn't. In the end, he fessed up. She was devastated – not so much about the financial troubles she had been kept in the dark about, but that her husband didn't feel he could tell her what was going on. They took out a second mortgage but got caught in the housing crisis, and they have yet to recover fully. Their house was eventually sold in a short sale. They've managed to stay in the community, but as renters, and they've had to move several times. I'm happy to say they are still married.

WHO'S BRINGING HOME THE BACON?
(AT LEAST ON PLAN A)

Bonnie, a mother of two who works in accounting, unexpectedly had the discussion early in her relationship with her now-husband. "I remember the dinner. I think the restaurant was called Caliente, on the Upper East Side. Mexican. Across a small table, wine before the meal. A nice date! We had been dating long enough that I suppose we had broached our status and agreed to something regarding long-term potential and kids. Over the wine he said, just by the way, 'I'm not the kind of guy who would be able to support the whole family.' I said to him, 'I get it. I wouldn't want that, anyway.'

I meant it! I still do, in terms of the independence. Even though it's hard. But I guess it could always be harder! Bottom line, I'm glad I went in eyes wide open. And I'm impressed he had the kahunas to say it."

That discussion was a reality check. It headed off future resentment when Bonnie may have wanted to stay home. She knew the deal going in.

It doesn't matter what you decide, but it's important that you make a decision. And if all goes well, you can stick to that decision.

HAVE A BACKUP PLAN

People lose jobs. Companies fail. Stuff happens. If you decide to be dependent on one income, always try to have the non-working spouse stay up-to-date on some kind of money-making skill set. Keep the resume fresh.

DIVIDE AND CONQUER

Decide who will do what with the finances – but always keep each other informed. For example, one person could be in charge of budgeting and making sure you don't overspend. The other might be in charge of keeping track of tax-related stuff.

LIGHTEN THE LOAD BY AUTOMATING

Consider automating your financial management in a single place. Mint is a great free online resource to keep track of where you're spending money. Other options include Mvelopes and Learnvest. But always remember that when something is free, you are the product. Many sites sell your information or get a commission if you buy a product promoted on the website.

CROWDSOURCE ADVICE

Discreetly ask experienced friends whom you respect what works for them. You don't need to know what each one makes or any financial details. But it always helps to get other opinions on what works.

BE FULLY AWARE OF THE COST OF DIVORCE

Splitting up is often the most devastating financial decision you can make. A number of friends have come to me asking for advice regarding divorce, since I went through a painful split at age 30. I listen to their reasons and ask a lot of questions. Very often a lot of the frustration, when you get down to it, has to do with one spouse not living up to the financial and lifestyle expectations that the couple started out with. There is resentment.

Madison came to me asking about divorce. When she and her husband met, things were great. He was enjoying a successful career on Wall Street. She had a part-time freelance career. They got married and had kids. They mutually decided that he would leave his job and start his own hedge fund. It was touch and go for a while, as it is with many new businesses. He had a great track record and had some really good days. But he lost money. Outside investors dried up. He continued to try to make a go of the hedge fund and refused to give up his dream. Tensions over money started to take over their relationship. He suggested she work full time.

That wasn't what she had signed up for. In her mind she didn't want to miss her kids growing up, and that was what he was asking her to do.

She confided that she was thinking of leaving. I asked her: If a big deal came though, and you had absolutely no financial worries ever again, would you still leave? She wasn't sure. Then I asked her to play out what happens to her situation financially if she leaves as things currently stand. Their assets were already depleted. She would absolutely have to work full time, so that right there largely defeats the purpose. She would get very little, if any, financial support from her ex because there simply wasn't anything there. And as a single, full-time working mother, she would have a lot less time with her kids.

Keep in mind that there was no abuse and no cheating. This was really about money and lifestyle and the tensions surrounding disappointment and financial struggles. I'm happy to report that Madison is still married. Things have improved just a bit financially, but they're still not ideal. But because she saw that divorce didn't really solve what was upsetting her, she made the choice to keep her family together and avoid making what I believe would have been a mistake.

———

Stuff happens – be prepared

———

RISA GOLDBERG & LESLIE VENOKUR

- CO-FOUNDERS AND CO-CEO'S, BIG CITY MOMS

OUR FINANCIAL GROWNUP MOMENT

While in a cab rushing off to a business meeting for our corporate jobs, there was a talk show on the radio. The topic was work/life balance. The interviewee made a comment . . . Little Kids, Little Problems. Big Kids, Big Problems. Meaning that when your kids are younger the issues that arise are about sleep, feeding, meeting those milestones that new parents stress about. As your kids get older you are dealing with relationships, school work, and all the extra-curricular stuff. It really made us think.

We started Big City Moms 12 years ago as a side/fun business while we both had corporate, full-time jobs. In the back of our minds we had hoped that it would someday turn into a profitable business that could replace our "real" jobs at the time and allow us some flexibility.

Five years into the business we decided to leave the corporate world and work at Big City Moms full time, to give us flexibility while building a company that we believed in. As sisters, we had a great support system, which we believe was also key to making the big leap.

Big City Moms is a national company now and requires us both to travel often to attend various events. But we feel like we are in a groove, and technology has allowed us to continue to be present for our families.

OUR LESSON TO SHARE

We both have always had a strong work ethic that definitely came from our father, who always worked hard. He was always there for all the important family moments.

As your kids get older they require more attention. Working a corporate job, traveling to speak at conferences, or setting up boutiques in our corporate jobs was very rewarding. However, realizing that our children would need us to be involved in their day-to-day activities even more as they got older motivated us to work harder to build our own company. It allows us the flexibility to work from home, make our own schedules, and to run to school functions if needed. We encourage others to find a way to build their careers in a way that complements their family's needs, and get the best of both worlds.

CHOOSE HOW YOU WANT TO BALANCE
WORK AND LIFE

EVERYONE HAS HAD or will have a moment when they have to make a conscious decision about how to handle their work and family life – if they want to have a family. It doesn't have to be balanced. You may choose to focus heavily on one or the other.

For example, the main breadwinner of the house, historically the man, but not always these days, may spend a higher percentage of his or her time focused on work. The other partner may spend more time on the family. It doesn't have to be balanced, it just has to be what works.

In Risa and Leslie's case, running their own business gave them the freedom to choose specific times they wanted to spend with their kids, such as school events. They weren't always working less, but they got to choose how they worked. The reality is that for many people, being an entrepreneur can mean less time for family.

Risa and Leslie's story is a common one. Many women, and increasingly men, make changes to their professional situations when they become parents to add more flexibility to their schedules.

WORK/LIFE BALANCE

According to author and writer Susie Orman Schnall, the struggle with work/life balance is all too real. Susie has talked to over 100 working women for her interview series The Balance Project.

Susie found that there isn't one single approach that works across the board for all women to find balance. But there are strategies that can work for many women. Here's her advice:

Reject Perfection

Accept that you can't do it all perfectly all the time, and that perfection serves no purpose in your life. Believing the images you see on Pinterest and Facebook, and buying into the media's portrayal of the elusive ideal of balance, will only set you up to feel inadequate. Sheryl Sandberg says it best in *Lean In:* "Done is better than perfect."

Spread It Out

Life has a way of presenting itself in phases, and you shouldn't expect to be spectacular at everything on a daily basis. So rather than thinking that each day needs to have a healthy balance of work, family, and self, it's more realistic to try to balance those things out over a few weeks, or a few months, or whatever time frame works best for you. Check in with yourself after that period of time and assess how you're doing with all that's on your plate. Make changes and adjust if necessary.

Say No

Many parents practically brag about how busy they are, as if it's a badge of honor. Sure, parent's lives are, by nature, busy. But we owe it to ourselves to say no sometimes and take care of our own needs because "me" time is not selfish, it's necessary. We don't need to keep piling more and more unnecessary things on top of the have to's in our lives just to look and feel important. Because being crazy busy does *not* make us look and feel important. It makes us look and feel frazzled.

Be open to making changes that will enhance your life since these changes will ultimately lead to making you a better employee, mother, wife, friend, etc.

THE BENEFITS (LITERALLY) OF GOING CORPORATE

We touched on this in the previous chapter, but I'd like to emphasize this: When it comes to families, a corporate job, with regular hours and a steady paycheck, can be a great choice. Many companies have incredible support systems for families, especially moms.

And, recently, the working world has gotten a lot better.

Working Mother editorial director Jennifer Owens tells me, "Thirty years ago, the gold standard was an on-site facility, and seven of the Best Companies offered it. Today, all Best Companies feature an array of child-care benefits because they know how important it is to working parents, from backup and sick-child care to business travel reimbursements, summer camps, and, yes, actual daily child care."

And speaking of child care, doing the math when a maternity (or paternity!) leave ends can be very shortsighted. In many cases women stop working because when you add up the cost of going to work, which includes child care, transportation, work wardrobe, and so on, they actually lose money going to work. Based on that, they stay home.

But here's the catch: If you can find a way to make it work financially, going back to work may pay off in the long term. It could be part time. You may be able to work some days at home, or at least avoid travel. Be creative with your company.

One of the key reasons women make less later in their careers than men is that they take a break. The same will likely be true for men as more fathers choose to stay home. Even if you work fewer days or in a less-demanding job at your company for a little while, staying, in some capacity, will almost always pay off financially.

Reuters agreed to allow me to work a 4-day week when my son was born. At times those four days were very long, 12-hour marathons when the company had cutbacks during the recession and my unit was stretched. I was responsible for making sure a freelancer was in my seat on Fridays, and thankfully all went well.

Build you career in a way that complements your family's needs

I turned down countless opportunities, including all travel assignments. I attended no networking functions after work for years, always rushing home to put my son to bed.

I turned down major interviews with very important CEOs and business leaders if they happened on a Friday, for fear of setting a precedent. I'll never forget my heart sinking when I had to turn down an interview with the then-head of Microsoft, Steve Ballmer. My colleague did a great job, but it was so hard to watch.

The choice I made slowed down my career, but I persevered. And by the way, I did finally interview Ballmer a few years later. I still remember the great chat we had about our kids' love of Xbox while the crew was setting up.

Years later I'm back to working five days a week. It's exhausting at times. But I look back and I'm proud of all I've accomplished despite spending some time on the so-called mommy track, raising my son and helping to raise my two teenage stepchildren. I lead my unit at Reuters, write an internationally syndicated personal finance column, and continue to interview the top financial leaders in the world. I even finally found time for that personal finance book I always wanted to write!

I've also benefitted from having strong parents who did plenty of financial planning for themselves, although I've resisted efforts to be informed about those plans. I want to stay the child. But my friend Elle Kaplan's story has been a great motivator to me, and hopefully will be to you, to start asking more questions about estate planning and being aware of parents' wishes.

ELLE KAPLAN

- CEO AND FOUNDING PARTNER, LEXION CAPITAL

MY FINANCIAL GROWNUP MOMENT

As an undergraduate in college I studied English and chemistry, so it's fair to say that, at that point in my life, a career in wealth management was not really on my radar. I grew up in a pretty traditional family with a working father and a stay-at-home mom. My mother – a brilliant woman – dedicated her life to raising the four of us, and left my father to work and handle the family's finances, not uncommon for many American families. During my junior year in college, my father grew ill and very suddenly fell into a deep coma. I remember, clearly, waking up one morning to find my mother crying at the kitchen table: she was grief-stricken and completely overwhelmed with my family's finances. I witnessed her struggle to find a trustworthy advisor, so I started to do some research. I realized that, when handling personal savings and investments, Wall Street very rarely put clients first. Wall Street is overwhelmingly made up of brokerages whose primary job is to sell you something in the best interests of themselves. Most of America doesn't have access to high-quality, client-centric wealth management advice.

This means that there was an entire population of people who – like my mother – had nowhere to turn when it came to getting honest advice about their finances. My family's experience planted a seed, and my career path was forever changed.

At 22 years old and with $200 in my pocket, I moved to New York with the dream of changing an industry from self-serving to serving the best interests of people like my mom. For a while I struggled, working as a temp doing basic office work and applying to different Wall Street firms in my spare time. I was rejected a lot, but I did not give up. I held on to my mother's experience and my dream of making a difference. I was finally given a chance at a firm when a company I interviewed for as a receptionist noticed my A average and gave

> *Make sure that what you do is good enough for your mom*

me a shot as an analyst. Fast-forward twelve years later, following a successful Wall Street career and an MBA from Columbia University, I launched LexION Capital: the first woman-owned, woman-run wealth management firm. Today, as CEO and founder, I work each day to build a more-inclusive, more-responsible Wall Street for all.

MY LESSON TO SHARE

We are all given a choice in how we view our personal and professional hardships. How we deal with them and what we learn from them is what is most significant. Rather than approaching my family's hardships from a negative perspective, I was inspired to create an investment firm that would keep the interests of everyone – and especially women like my mother – a priority. To this day the ethos at LexION is: "Is this investment advice good enough for my mom?" My mother's experience is, I've learned, not uncommon. Her journey is something I have carried with me through my time on Wall Street, and is what inspired me to found the only woman-run, woman-owned wealth management firm. Providing transparent financial investment advice is, to me, one of the most effective ways to empower women. Helping someone obtain financial independence is the first step to keeping them safe. It's why I do what I do.

HAVING THE CHAT – WITH YOUR PARENTS

PART OF BEING a grownup is realizing that your parents may not have their act together financially. Like Elle, young people often find themselves thrown into their parents' financial crisis, often with no warning. Out of the blue Elle not only had to deal with her dying father but with a mother who had, effectively, never become a financial grownup.

This is one of the toughest talks you'll probably ever have with your parents. It feels invasive to ask about their finances. But if one parent is in the dark financially, as was the case with Elle, you'll probably be the one coming to the rescue. And if both are financially irresponsible, you may end up supporting them at some point.

ESTATE PLANNING

The other takeaway from Elle's experience is that there wasn't any estate planning going on with her parents. If there was, her mother was in the dark. Again, it almost doesn't matter what the plan is, as long as there is a plan. There are plenty of online legal resources to draft a quick will, and file it somewhere safe. More importantly, let others know where your assets are and what your wishes are. Elle's mother didn't even know what her own assets and liabilities were!

According to a recent Wells Fargo/Harris Poll, one quarter of all affluent investors feel uncomfortable talking to family about estate plans. The reality is that many of us don't even know whether our parents are in fact affluent, or what their financial situation is. We need to open the lines of communication so we can be there for them when they need us to be. And so we can be ready when they're no longer there for us.

YOUR DIGITAL LEGACY

One final note: When taking account of your assets, don't forget your digital assets, including social media accounts. Make sure your wishes are known so relatives can access priceless memories accumulated over the years. Many social media companies have set up ways to pass on social media accounts. For example, Facebook allows you to go into your security settings and designate a legacy contact. You may even want to designate a digital executor for you and your relatives as well. Take the time to fill out your wishes, and make sure that the people you care about do so as well.

YOUR FINANCIAL GROWNUP CHECKLIST
～ FAMILY ～

- ✓ Stay engaged in your family finances.
- ✓ Your spouse is your financial partner – choose carefully!
- ✓ Divorce cuts assets in half.
- ✓ The mommy/daddy track is still a track.
- ✓ Corporations can be more family-friendly than going solo.
- ✓ No one lives forever: have the talk.
- ✓ Make a plan for your digital legacy, and your family's.

CHAPTER SEVEN

CONSIDER YOUR REAL ESTATE OPTIONS

D EALING WITH REAL ESTATE on some level is 100 percent un-avoidable if you want to be a financial grownup. You can live with your parents and avoid it temporarily. That may even be the best financial move if, for example, you have a student loan to pay off. But eventually you should have your own home. When the time comes, start running the numbers on renting vs. buying and also on investment vs. just a place to live. Of course, that requires thoughtful planning. The Role Models in this chapter all made decisions that were unexpected and risky but, at the same time, well-thought-out and sensible. Learn from them, and then really think about your priorities and your options given your resources.

Don't buy a house just because it seems like the grownup thing to do, but don't rent just because it's easier. Think about what's right for you now and in the foreseeable future. The answers might surprise you. They surprised Spencer Rascoff, one of the most well-respected voices in real estate today, whose story caught me totally off-guard.

SPENCER RASCOFF

- CEO, ZILLOW
- AUTHOR, *NEW YORK TIMES* BEST SELLER, *ZILLOW TALK*

MY FINANCIAL GROWNUP MOMENT

My financial grownup moment came when my wife and I first moved to Seattle in 2003. We needed somewhere to live. But we weren't ready to buy a home and were looking to rent. We came across the perfect place, but the owner wanted to sell, and not to rent. The house had been on the market for about a year, so we figured the owner was having a tough time selling it at the price he wanted. We wrote him a letter and convinced him to rent it to us instead. Since he was paying a mortgage out of his own pocket, and was facing dropping the price to sell it at a loss, he agreed. It was a win-win.

A year later, while living in the rental, we learned my wife was expecting our first child. Now it was really grownup time. There's a lot of social pressure when you are starting a family to own a home. Plus, Zillow was just getting off the ground, and as an executive of an online real estate company it dawned on me that I should probably own a home. But we were happy in our rented home. So we offered to buy the home from our landlord. Again, it was unusual, but it worked!

A few years later, when our second child was born, we decided to look for a bigger house. It was a terrible time for the housing market and a bad time to be a seller. So we did exactly what the previous owner had done: We found a couple that wanted to rent the house with the option of eventually buying it later. I still own that house today.

MY LESSON TO SHARE

If we'd let the "For Sale" sign on that house scare us away when we were looking to rent, we would have missed out on a really great opportunity. Instead, our first successful real estate adventure expanded our sense of what's possible and encouraged us to keep exploring that gray area between for sale and not for sale. Since then, we've continued to buy and sell through somewhat unconventional methods.

It's important you think of buying a house as buying a place to live, not as an investment you expect to appreciate. You should love where you live and make the decision to buy or rent based on your personal and financial circumstances. With that being said, buying is not right for everyone. It's important to focus on your time horizon when deciding whether to buy or rent. It all depends on your specific circumstances, where you live, and how long you're planning to stay there.

So even though we tend to think that owning a home is always the right thing when you have kids, finding a nice rental may be the better option if you live in an expensive city like New York or San Francisco.

SOME ADVICE ON BUYING A HOME

SPENCER'S POINT IS universal: real estate is not one size fits all. While owning your own home is considered the "grownup" thing to do, don't fall into the trap of buying a home just because you feel it's expected.

THINK CREATIVELY

Never be afraid to ask questions. Learn about the goals of the owner. Even if a home isn't for sale, the owner may be willing to sell it under the right circumstances. And if a home *is* for sale, you may be able to rent it anyway. Be persistent. Many times homes go on the market, a bid is accepted, and you may think that you've missed out on your dream house. But keep in touch – deals fall through all the time and homes come back on the market. Real estate is full of unexpected twists and turns, as Spencer points out.

THINK PERSONALLY

Put your needs first, and then see if you can make the finances work so that you can live where you want to live. That may mean renting to get into the best school district. That may mean doing a lot of research to get the best financing to buy a home. If you value having a large piece of property, you may choose to have a longer commute to work. But finding a home doesn't always mean making the huge financial decision to buy, just because of external pressure. If the CEO of Zillow can stand up for what's right for him, even if it goes against expectations, so can you.

START A DIALOGUE

If a home you love is priced too high, talk to the owners. Let them know you're interested if they can adjust the price. Or, like in Spencer's case, that you aren't ready to buy, but if they're willing, you could rent from them for a short period of time. If you do want to buy, there may be something that you're not aware of that could create more flexibility in the price. A friend of mine, while negotiating to buy an apartment, overheard the seller telling a friend that she couldn't wait to unload the property. So my friend knew that she could drive a hard bargain, and she got the apartment at a great price.

You should love where you live

BOBBI REBELL

- REUTERS TV ANCHOR AND COLUMNIST
- AUTHOR, *HOW TO BE A FINANCIAL GROWNUP*

MY FINANCIAL GROWNUP MOMENT

I started working at CNBC as a news associate in the 1990s. I had a tiny ground floor studio sublet on Manhattan's Upper West Side, paying about $900 a month in rent. I noticed that studios in the building were selling for about $100,000, and I started doing the math. Rates were about 8 percent. If I put down the required 20 percent for a co-op, my payments would be $587 a month, with a big tax deduction. I'd also have to pay building maintenance for a couple hundred dollars, but about half of that would be deductible. It would cost me a lot less money out-of-pocket to own than to rent.

But the real estate market was falling, and each time I looked at a studio to buy, the prices were getting lower. Would it be foolish for me, a single young woman just barely out of college, to buy an apartment that was likely to go down in value? And what if I got married? Or decided to move out of New York City to be a local news reporter?

I made a life decision to be an owner, not a renter. Cash flow-wise it was clearly a better deal in the short term, and I decided that the short-term benefit would make up for the fact that the apartment could very well go down in value in the long term. The risk was that I would have to sell it before it went back up in value. But I ended up living there for about seven years. In the end, the apartment I bought for $90,000, at age 23, sold for $250,000. After several other moves I have parlayed that investment into the three-bedroom Upper East Side condo I now live in with my family. We do have a mortgage, but the apartment has gone up in value since we bought it in 2007. Owning real estate has been a great life decision that has given me and my family financial freedom and security.

MY LESSON TO SHARE

Think about the life you want to have, your priorities, and while being cognizant of the market, make a choice. In my case, I was born in New York City, and that's where my family and friends were. I knew that even if I did take a job in another city, the odds were I would want to return to New York City where my roots were. It was home, and I wanted to be there. So being an owner with a long-term horizon made sense. Had I avoided making a decision, I would have missed the dip in the market that did come, but I also would not have had the upside, which allowed me to live my dream of raising a family in New York City, just blocks from where I was born.

Make a decision

FIGURE OUT WHAT'S RIGHT FOR YOU

JUST BECAUSE SOMETHING seems like a great deal, it doesn't mean it's right for you. The one-size-fits-all American dream of owning one's own home, with the white picket fence and the two-car garage in the suburbs, has been turned on its head in recent years. Bigger is no longer always better, and housing has become more individual.

The key is to figure out what's right for you and then make a decision. The economic recession forced many young people to postpone that decision. In many cases they weren't in a strong enough financial position to be making decisions about whether to buy or rent. They were living at home with mom and dad. Now that's changing.

In the past the general thinking was to stretch to buy the biggest home for which you could qualify and grow into it. Now many new home buyers want smaller, more-affordable homes, without the excesses and financial burdens of the past. We all saw so many dreams die in the housing bust. As a result many people simply aren't driven to own a lot of stuff, and therefore they don't need big houses to hold all their possessions.

THE DOWN PAYMENT: WHERE TO GO TO GET THE CASH

That's a tough one for millions of aspiring home-owners, but one that can be solved with a little creativity and a hard look at the resources that could be used to get that home. That's something PwC's Bob Moritz took to heart. Here's his story.

BOB MORITZ

• GLOBAL CHAIRMAN OF PwC

MY FINANCIAL GROWNUP MOMENT

Nineteen eighty-five was a big year for me . . . I graduated from college, got a job at Price Waterhouse, and got married. To celebrate my new life as an official grownup, I went out and bought myself a Firebird. I had worked hard to get through college and the Firebird was both a reward for my hard work and a lot of fun to drive. I loved that car . . . but I also learned that having a sports car was expensive. Between car payments, insurance, and gas, I was starting to feel squeezed. Plus, I was starting to learn that other stuff was expensive too – stuff like rent. And as an official grownup, and one half of a married couple planning to start a family, it was time to be thinking in terms of mortgage payments, not rent. So I sold the Firebird and bought a rusty Datsun B210 for $500. I won't say that it didn't cost me a pang, but I really did see it as an investment in the future. That transaction put me in a position where I could afford the down payment on a co-op apartment, and start building toward a more solid financial future.

135

I don't see that Firebird as an indulgence . . . and I wouldn't call it a phase, either. It was a perfectly fine choice to make at the time. But different choices were called for later.

MY LESSON TO SHARE

You choose what you let go of, just as you choose what you reach for.

WHAT YOU NEED TO CONSIDER IN BUYING A HOME

ONE OF THE biggest impediments to home ownership is that elusive down payment. But many people have the resources somewhere, if they make it a priority, as Bob Moritz did.

Many young home owners will tell you they were saving up right out of college – living at home and passing on some, though not all, of those fun nights out with their friends – in order to bank money for that down payment. It's a tough choice, but it's a choice that creates options.

ASSESS YOUR OPTIONS – INCLUDING LOCATION, LOCATION, LOCATION

The good news is that, with the technology available today, many jobs can be done remotely. In fact, quite a few companies encourage workers to be based in home offices, to save the company rent! That creates a whole new level of flexibility when it comes to choosing a place to live. Just because you get a job in a major city doesn't mean you can't live somewhere a lot cheaper – and in many cases get the same big-city salary. Even if you work for a local company, settling down in a more affordable area can be an instant way to have a higher quality of life.

The reality is that, until recently, most millennials didn't have a lot of options when it came to housing. They could watch their small paychecks vaporize paying rent they could barely afford, or live at home with mom and dad and try to save up while putting their grownup lives on hold. In that case, living at home was often the smarter financial decision.

DON'T LET THE FUTURE STOP THE PRESENT

Think realistically about where you want to be in five years. One roadblock that hampers young people is that the future is so wide open. I remember thinking: what happens if I get married to my boyfriend? What will happen to the apartment then? Well, I did get married, and we lived there! Had I been forced to sell it at a loss, I knew, from the math that I had done, that most likely I would have saved enough on the monthly carrying costs to cushion any possible losses. But it was a risk.

Financial resources are also a big component. If you want to be a buyer and don't have the financial resources for a down payment, get a plan together. Obviously the best ways to save are to raise your top line (what you earn) and lower your bottom line (what you spend). That means focusing on earning the most money you can and lowering your costs as much as possible.

That may mean a side hustle, as we talked about earlier. It may mean roommates. It may mean selling something you love, as Bob Moritz did. If you have any rent-free options, such as living at home, consider yourself lucky. But have a timeline and an exit strategy. Living at home or with roommates indefinitely is not a grownup move.

CONSIDER YOUR RISK TOLERANCE

What your risks are depend on your situation. If you rent you're protected from a housing downturn. Your rent may even go down! But, of course, you often have no control over how much a landlord can raise the rent. I have friends who are raising families in apartments that they've been in for years, who live in fear of the yearly lease and the possibility of having to uproot their families. When rent goes up in one apartment it's usually part of a broader trend in the area, so it's tough to get a better deal without leaving the community.

But as we've seen in the housing crisis, buying has its own set of risks. Many folks bought at the top of the market and found themselves in houses worth less than they owed. If they could pay their mortgage, they were okay. But many were experiencing their own financial hardship, and being locked into houses they couldn't afford only made things worse. They couldn't downsize. And if a job opportunity came up that required a move, that house that they couldn't sell became a very heavy ball and chain.

I interviewed countless well-meaning folks during the housing crisis. These were educated, middle-class homeowners who knew exactly what they were doing when they bought their homes. They borrowed responsible amounts of money and had solid jobs. But things fell apart anyway because of events that were beyond their control. They took a risk, had bad luck, and paid dearly for it. Many are renters today.

DO THE MATH

Add up your current cost of living. Not just the rent or mortgage payment, but what it costs to be in your neighborhood, state, and region of the country. I'm amazed at the "discounts" I get at stores simply by leaving New York City. Add up what you spend each month on everything, including gas and car payments if you live in a place where you have to drive, or public transportation costs if you live in an urban area. Factor in landscaping if you have to take care of a lawn, or maintenance costs if you live in a housing development. Think about what you're saving if you have free cable in a rental. Or what expenses you don't have to pay because you have roommates. Develop an accurate picture of what you spend now compared to what it would cost where you'd like to live.

Then take out a calculator and add it all up. The number may be a little rough around the edges, but it may reveal some truths you hadn't thought of.

For example, many people assume the suburbs are cheaper than the city in the New York Metro area. And this can be true if you're looking at the fancy TriBeCa lofts featured in the media. Millions of people live in more modest apartments that have prices comparable to suburban homes. And when you start doing detailed calculations and include lawn care, the cost of having multiple cars, time and money related to commuting to jobs, and the overall maintenance of a suburban house, you may find that living in the city is no more expensive than living in the suburbs. You have to do the math.

The good news is that interest rates are at historic lows these days. While they're likely to go up in the next few years, they should remain well below the 8 percent levels I faced in the 1990s and the 18 percent my parents faced in the early 1980s. Depending on your income, you may qualify for loans where the required down payment is far lower than the standard 20 percent, though you will likely have to pay mortgage insurance. There's more transparency and information out there than ever before – it's become a great time to grow up and have a home of your own.

*You choose what you let go of,
just as you choose what you reach for*

SUSIE GHARIB

- SENIOR SPECIAL CORRESPONDENT
  FORTUNE MAGAZINE
- CNBC CONTRIBUTOR

MY FINANCIAL GROWNUP MOMENT

Buying a co-op apartment in the height of New York City's financial crisis in the 1970s. I was 26, newly married, and my husband and I invested almost all of our savings into buying a small apartment that needed to be completely renovated. It was a scary time to be investing in New York City real estate. The future was bleak and there was no guarantee of making money on the purchase. The city was on the verge of bankruptcy and President Gerald Ford refused to approve bailout money to stave off financial collapse. Remember that famous *Daily News* headline: "Ford to New York: Drop Dead." Adding to the anxiety, oil prices spiked and there were long lines to get gasoline. The maintenance fees for co-ops surged dramatically because of those higher fuel costs, so many New Yorkers fled Manhattan, selling their apartments in landmark buildings at bargain prices.

That's when we made our first big investment as a couple. Even though real estate prices plummeted, they were still steep for us. It was a stretch on our budget given I was just starting my career as a journalist and my husband was a newly-minted Wall Street financial analyst. But we were eager to own a home, and so we took the plunge and the responsibility that went with it. We were now on the hook for a 30-year mortgage and monthly payments. It was a serious commitment. So we were ruthless about all our expenditures. We walked to work or took the bus – no more taxis. And did all the apartment renovations ourselves – plastering, painting, and plumbing. By contrast, most of my friends were not yet married, let alone thinking about mortgage payments or budgets. For the first time in my life I felt so grown up and responsible.

But it was worth it. New York City survived. Economic growth returned. Owning New York property made sense again. And by the early 1980s, when we had to move to a bigger place to accommodate our growing family, we sold that apartment for ten times more than we paid for it! It turned out to be the best investment ever and established us on a solid financial foundation.

MY LESSON TO SHARE

It's not enough to save money – you have to invest it. You will live longer than your parents, so you will need more money – for yourself, your children's education, and your retirement. It seems like a long way off, but it isn't really. Don't be intimidated by the jargon of 401(k)s, index funds, Roth IRAs. Ask questions and get started – now. You'll be happy you did.

You will grow up and live somewhere that will probably involve making a payment whether it is rent or a mortgage. You may not want to, but you will. Make a grownup decision based on your assets, goals, and desired lifestyle sooner rather than later. Getting into the real estate market early almost always will pay off, if you choose your home wisely. Renting can be a good choice, if you go in with your eyes open and know the risks. You will probably spend more hours in your home over your lifetime than anywhere else. Be a decider.

OWNERSHIP ISN'T ALWAYS BEST

THINK ABOUT WHAT matters most. One regret I have from locking into home ownership at such an early age is that I didn't get to live in different neighborhoods in New York City. I never got to live in a loft in Soho (though with my budget it would have come with several roommates). And forget ever trying out trendy Brooklyn.

You may have a career that demands moving every few years. You may have friends you actually enjoy living with. You may have a great rent-stabilized apartment. You may be very focused on your career and not want to make the time investment needed to find and finance a home to buy. And you may simply not have the down payment. But make that decision a deliberate one.

One young woman I spoke with, Jenny, lives in a five-bedroom apartment in Brooklyn. Her roommates consist of a revolving door of 20-somethings who found the apartment on Craigslist, which is how she found it. The problem is that she is no longer a 20-something – she is now in her early 30s. Thanks to a modest inheritance for several years she has had the financial means to buy her own apartment. But her inability to make a decision to move is starting to take a toll. The real estate market has been climbing, and what she can afford has been falling.

Living in the post-college multi-roommate situation impacts her whole life. Dating is hard enough in New York City, but to have a gaggle of roommates like that can look juvenile to guys she dates. If you ask her she'll say that she is thinking about buying an apartment. This has been going on for the better part of a decade. She fails to realize that her inability to make a decision *is* a decision. Buying a home is simply not a priority for her even though, with her financial means and stable job, it's probably the best financial move.

DO WHAT'S RIGHT FOR YOU

One of my younger colleagues came to me for advice a year or so ago about her living situation. She had just won a lottery for middle-class New Yorkers and was being offered subsidized housing. She was excited but confused. The new apartment was a large one-bedroom, in a brand new building. But it was far from work and was actually much more expensive than the small Manhattan apartment she was living in.

We talked about what was important to her. She loved being close to all of her friends. They went out to restaurants and shows and concerts, and she had a great New York City lifestyle for a young, single woman. The new apartment would be a one-hour subway ride away. She would be cash-strapped and would have to cut back on doing all the things she loved about living in New York City. Her current apartment was tiny and cramped, and in terrible shape. Then again, for the Upper West Side, the rent was reasonable, and it was affordable for her. She turned down the fancier apartment.

Real estate is not one size fits all. Everyone has different priorities. Don't make a move just because it seems like you should. Live the life you want, where you want.

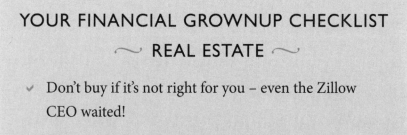

YOUR FINANCIAL GROWNUP CHECKLIST
~ REAL ESTATE ~

- ✓ Don't buy if it's not right for you – even the Zillow CEO waited!

- ✓ Start small if you do want to be an owner, but start.

- ✓ Find a way to get the down payment, even if it means selling something.

- ✓ Don't make cost assumptions about location – do the math.

- ✓ Financially, buying real estate early in life usually pays off as an investment, but you have to live the investment. Literally.

CHAPTER EIGHT

MIXING FRIENDS AND FINANCES

TAKE A LOOK at some of the most successful businesses of the last few decades, and it's clear that friends working together is often a formula for success. Facebook was started by a bunch of friends at Harvard. Microsoft was also started by friends, as was Apple. But in almost every case the business changed the friendship dynamic, and hard decisions had to be made. It's rare that the group of friends smiling in someone's home in the early days is still together when the big money starts rolling in.

The fact is that mixing friends and money can have huge financial benefits as well as unintended consequences. It's a minefield. Much like with a marriage, working together often seems rosy at the start, but when things get messy relationships are tested and brutal decisions have to be made.

AARON SHAPIRO

• CEO, HUGE INC.

MY FINANCIAL GROWNUP MOMENT

When I was 24 years old I launched Silverpop out of my apartment. It was my second entrepreneurial venture but the first time where I was not only responsible for the well-being of the company, but also the future of my employees, who were really my friends. We ended up raising over $30 million in funding, but when the dot.com crash hit I quickly had to reassess our business strategy. While there was still money in the bank, after calculating business expenses and overhead I realized we were going to run out of funds within a year. I had to make a tough decision. Doing what was right for the business would mean laying off a number of friends. I'm not going to lie; it was a tough decision that I agonized over for a while. In the end I chose to move forward with the layoffs in order to save the business – which not only allowed for the company to thrive, but also resulted in a stronger team of employees.

MY LESSON TO SHARE

My biggest lesson learned was that it's critical to be honest with yourself about the situation your company is really in – no matter how hard that reality might seem. As an entrepreneur you have to be able to do what's best for your company even when that's personally hard.

Be honest with yourself

I also learned not to get swept up in all of the hype that typically comes along with launching a company. When you start out and are looking for funding, one of the first questions VCs will ask you is how many people you employ. It's tempting to over-hire in order to appear more substantial than you really are – but ultimately, the leaner your business is, the better.

BE CAREFUL MIXING FRIENDS AND WORK

AARON'S EXPERIENCE IS something countless entrepreneurs can relate to: mixing business and friendship. He hired his friends, and then found himself in a real mess.

We spend so much time at work that there's a natural tendency to want to be with our friends, and also to give them opportunities. But there are endless examples of sticky situations.

The recent huge success of GoPro when it initially went public is one example. Founder Nick Woodman is perhaps the poster boy for friendship loyalty. His first employee at the company was his

149

college roommate, Neil Dana. When the company started, Wood-man promised to pay his friend 10 percent of any proceeds he got from selling company shares. The gentlemen's agreement ended up costing Woodman more than $200 million out of his own pocket soon after the company went public. But he did right by his friend, and stuck to the deal. Neil Dana is still a part of the company, as the director of music and specialty.

THE HAVES AND THE HAVE NOTS

The above example also points out that not all friends will be equally financially successful in life. We may all start out on the same path, but as we move through the various stages in our career, different paths emerge, along with different priorities.

We also may find ourselves at different levels from our peers at points in our career. For example, one of my supervisors from early in my career at CNBC, has actually worked for me at Reuters! We've become great friends over the years, and we laugh about it, but it can still be a bit strange for me.

DOING BUSINESS WITH FRIENDS

Hiring friends to help out even outside the office can be a minefield. So what do you do if you need to hire someone – not necessarily a job, but for something personal. For example, you're putting to-gether a website to show off your photography. You have a friend who designed web pages as their side hustle. Perfect match, right? Not so fast. It will get complicated fast, so go in with your eyes open.

First, you'll probably expect a "friends" discount. But your friend will be doing the same work they did for others. So is it right for them to be paid less? At the same time, they might have real clients who they would reasonably serve first. But you wouldn't want your project to take a backseat.

The upside of hiring a friend: They'll likely be more committed to the project because they care about you and are vested in your success. If all goes well it will bring you closer, and you'll have a lot of fun.

The downside: They may not do a great job, or you may disagree about something, which could do serious damage to the friendship.

Overall, tread carefully. Be realistic and open about expectations. The benefits often don't outweigh the risks. But if you do feel that your friend is the absolute best person for the job, be sure to lay out, ideally in writing, exactly what's expected, including payment and time frame of delivery.

Working with a friend isn't the place to bargain-hunt. Pay your friend fairly and on time. And realize that if you don't like the job they do, you may have to just let it go and move on in order to preserve the relationship. And that could cost you more money in the end.

SOCIAL MEDIA AT WORK – USE DISCRETION

Mixing your personal life and professional life is a challenge made more extreme by the emergence – and often urgent call – of social media. It may not be realistic to shut down our smart phone at work, but make it something that's in the background, that your boss and coworkers are unaware of.

A recent study from Listen found that 89 percent of Millennials ages 18 to 34 texted with family and friends during work hours. This isn't grownup behavior. That same survey found that 59 percent checked their social media accounts at work. It gets worse – 17 percent took selfies at work. The worst offenders according to the Listen survey? Those who work in IT and finance.

You're being paid to work. Our personal and work lives have blended, and unfortunately it's not a fair situation in most cases. Your boss probably expects you to be reachable via your smartphone 24/7. So you're expected to work during your personal time. But, while it's unfair, that same boss probably doesn't want to see your personal life happening at all during the primary work hours. Shutting off isn't realistic, but being discreet about it is.

Don't take out your phone during a client meeting, even if you urgently need to check on a personal matter. Excuse yourself to go to the restroom, and check it there. No one will know.

Handling relationships and technology at work is a minefield. Erica Keswin, Founding Principal of OPR, a human capital consulting firm, has been studying this for years. She says that relationships at work will have a direct impact on your success, so being focused on them will pay off financially.

Keswin says that while it's nice to feel good about the people we spend so much time with, psychologist Ron Friedman and many other researchers have pointed out that our peers are the ones who can make or break our happiness, our productivity, our creativity, and our engagement at work. In other words: our success.

Being distracted by what's going on outside of the office is a lose-lose situation. Not only is device-checking unprofessional, it also alienates us from the people we work with – our work friends.

Keswin's solution? She says the best antidote to addictive FOMO (fear of missing out) is diving into whatever it is we're supposed to actually be doing. When we get the urge to tune in to our online lives, we can, instead, turn to the person next to us or to an unfinished project. We can ground ourselves in what it is we're actually being paid to do – work.

And the best part is that by slowing down and taking a breather from our digital relationships, we're developing a self-awareness that will add depth and authenticity to all of our relationships, including the ones that really impact our career.

Study after study has shown that meaningful relationships are good for everyone's bottom line.

FRIENDS + FINANCE OUTSIDE OF WORK

There are few things as rewarding as lifelong friendships, so it's important to be respectful of different friends' financial resources and priorities. Here are some scenarios, and tips on how to handle them:

The Awkward Money Ask

Sometimes friends ask for money, or you may consider asking friends for money. This is a minefield. Countless relationships are ruined in even the most well-intentioned situations. Just asking or being asked for money often permanently changes the dynamics of a friendship, so tread carefully.

When they ask

First and foremost, be sensitive. Think about why they are asking, and the specific situation. Is this a friend who is financially responsible but is in a truly unexpected circumstance, such as needing medical help for themselves or their family? Or is this an irresponsible friend looking for a handout? Have you seen this friend spending money on discretionary items, only to ask you to help finance a "passion project"? It happens more than you think.

Then think about the amount they are asking for and whether you can truly afford it. Your friends are likely unaware of your financial obligations and circumstances. They may not realize that when you don't join them at trendy restaurants it's because it's simply not in your budget. So don't blame them for assuming that you're in a position to help, even if you're not. Only you know your own finances. You can't help a friend financially if it puts you in a precarious situation.

You also may not want to create a situation where you are owed money from a friend or feel you are giving them handouts.

In general, it's best to avoid directly handing friends money; but if you do, be clear on the terms. If it's a loan, write down all expectations, including a payment schedule.

When you ask

In general, just don't. It opens up a Pandora's box of issues. If you are in a position of dire need, think carefully about how it will change the friendship. If possible, meet in person and approach carefully. Talk about your circumstance and see if they offer to help. If you do ask outright, be ready for an uncomfortable situation. They may say that they want to think about it. Or that they want to talk to their significant other. If you do accept a loan, put everything in writing, and pay it back on time.

The Solution: The online group ask

There are wonderful new resources out there to ask for money from friends (and even strangers!) without putting anyone on the spot. For business ideas, there's Kickstarter. It allows you to efficiently ask large numbers of people for their support, and it has a clear reward available to those who are able to help you. I've supported many friend's campaigns and felt excited for them. I feel empowered to choose the amount I want to give, and I appreciate not being put on the spot. I also like to see how their project progresses, without having to ask in a way that sounds like I'm checking up on them. No guilt, lots of glory.

There are also great sites like GoFundMe.com which can be used for just about anything. I recently gave to the family of a colleague who has now passed away from cancer. When he got the diagnosis, his friends organized the campaign and spread the word through social media. The money poured in without the family having to "ask." I was able to think about what I wanted to give, discuss it with my husband, and make my donation in my own time. It was also an easy web-based transaction. Most of all, he and his family could see how many people were eager to help and support, both financially and emotionally, without having to ask. Hopefully it provided some comfort.

Sites like GoFundMe can also be used unapologetically for completely discretionary ventures. A friend's brother recently ran a campaign asking for friends to send him to the Super Bowl. It would have been way out of line to start asking friends in person for cash handouts for something like that, but a humorous online campaign where he was completely honest about the fact that he just wanted to go to the Super Bowl was great! Friends could send in their $10 donations and wish him well. No muss, no fuss, and lots of good humor. It may not be the primary mission of the site, but given the transparency, why not.

The Group Night Out

One of the most stressful financial times is the group dinner or night out. There's always the magnanimous friend who orders everything on the menu – then wants to split the check. And then the one who's struggling to make ends meet, pretending to not be hungry and ordering water.

The solution: control the bill from the start. The minute someone suggests any group outing that you'll be a part of, say you'll coordinate. Don't ask. Just do it. Immediately make a reservation at a place that fits your budget (or the one you feel will be most inclusive of the group's most budget-conscious members). Most people won't want to make waves, so it's a safe bet that everyone will follow your lead.

Check out the menu online in advance and have a plan

Think about the menu ahead of time – are there a couple of appetizers the group can share? Look at the wine list and research ahead of time. Call the restaurant and make sure they have what you want in stock.

Be the alpha guest

When you get there, take charge – and "sell" what you want to order. "I hear the best thing here is the calamari – how about we all share that as an appetizer?" etc.

Do the same thing with the wine– if you're confident in your selection, then everyone will be excited to try it. They won't be at all bothered that it's one of the least expensive choices. In fact, most of them will be very relieved when they get the bill.

The person who orders first sets the tone. It almost always follows that if the first one to order selects a fancy cocktail, an appetizer, and an entrée, most will follow suit, and the tab will then be much higher. Order first and skip the alcohol and appetizer, and I bet the bill will be smaller. It will also set you up as the person the waiter comes to.

By setting yourself up as the leader of the group, you can also control the dessert/coffee tab. Dessert can be a huge expense. If everyone orders a dessert, and then a fancy espresso drink, and even after-dinner drinks, the tab will balloon. But if you take charge, you can say, Hey, the desserts here are amazing, let's order a couple for the table to share. And when the waiter asks about coffee or tea, you can either say no, we'll pass, or say to the group, No one wants to be up all night with coffee, right? Or if you or the group really do want coffee, at least make it regular coffee. If you order an espresso drink first, the odds are high that your friends will take that as a cue to order something similar. Stick to the simple, less expensive coffee or tea. It's also less fattening!

Also make sure to say that you want the check as you order dessert – that move shuts down the tab. You may linger at the table, but you'll likely avoid having someone decide to start another round of after-dinner drinks. If the group wants to continue the evening, they'll likely go somewhere else for drinks, and you can join them or call it a night. But you remain in control of your own money, and probably no one will notice.

BYOB, but call first

I was recently shocked when my family had a celebratory dinner at a top New York City restaurant. When I got there, my brother-in-law offered me some of "his" wine. He had brought his own, a personal favorite, and the restaurant had put it in a decanter for him!

Now, bringing wine to this pricey restaurant was not inexpensive – they charged a $50 corkage fee. But let's do the math. Restaurants typically charge at least triple the price you would pay in a liquor store. At this restaurant, which was extremely expensive, many wines were over $100 a bottle. That same bottle would be about $33 in the store. Add the $50 fee and you still come out ahead.

Most restaurants charge a lot less to bring your own wine, generally between $10 and $20. Some don't charge at all! You'll typically save some money, and you'll always have the wine you want.

Be sure to call ahead and make sure you're allowed to bring your own wine. Also plan your selection and make sure it's not something on the restaurant's menu – bringing something they have available is considered bad form. You may save money, but bringing your own wine is supposed to be because you have a selection that's special to you.

This round's on me! NOT

Don't be the one who says "Drinks are on me." Ever. Treating everyone to a round of drinks sounds great when you do it. Everyone is your best friend. But if you can't afford it – or even if you can – just don't do it.

Date Stacking

Dating is expensive for both men and women.

For most women (and some men), dating involves a lot of often pricey prep. Buying the right clothing and shoes (not to mention dry cleaning, repairs, etc.). Then there's hair, makeup, often a manicure. All for what could be a total dud. Then the evening is shot and all that glamming up was for nothing.

My money-saving solution – stack two first dates in one night. Ideally one at 5 p.m. and one at 8 p.m. You get to meet two new people without having to get dressed up twice – everything does double duty.

Be honest but don't give details

Tell each date right upfront when you make the plans that you have a commitment at the other time, so there won't be any rudeness or misunderstandings. Always stress that you're so excited to meet them, and ask if it's okay that the date will end/begin when you arrange. If you only have one date, make it at 5 p.m., and say that you have to meet up with someone at 8 p.m.

If the date is a dud, you have a great out.

If the date is going super-well, then leaving your date wanting more isn't such a bad thing, is it?

For men, or whoever is treating or planning the evening, the date stacking is also a great money saver. There's no expectation of a long, drawn-out evening. You can plan a fun activity and then have drinks or a quick bite. Because the date is short, it's a lot easier to control the costs.

RSVP Reality Check

Who doesn't love a celebration? But when you get invited to a friend's birthday or bachelor/bachelorette party, the costs can spiral. The most important thing is to know what you're getting into so you can make a decision. Don't just blindly hit the yes button on the invitation!

Etiquette expert Lisa Taylor Richey advises you to get the details and then plan ahead and budget. Sometimes a relative is hosting and will be covering the cost completely – you just have to bring a present! But often a weekend getaway to celebrate a milestone can turn into a major financial commitment.

Find out, for example: how many meals out will you be expected to pay for for the friend who's having the birthday? Expect to pay your part and maybe more. Is everyone paying their own way, plus splitting the costs of the one who's having the birthday. Is there a group gift? Is there anything you can opt out of? Communication is key.

And what if you're part of the group in charge? Planning a bridal shower for a friend can turn into a big financial commitment. Budget and plan accordingly.

Richey says that if you're planning a party with your friends, plan how you're going to split the details. Are you going to keep a running total and split at the end, or are you each going to be responsible for certain aspects of the event? Will you negotiate a total fixed cost and pay ahead of time?

Run the event like a project at work. Put the details on paper and plan it. Then make sure everyone is on board.

Tough Love

Sometimes you get invited to an event that, no matter how much you try to justify the cost, you just can't afford. Certified Financial Planner Shannah Compton Game says the best money strategy is to make sure that you have a budget in place so you know how much you can spend. Then set a limit on your fun (for example, I can only spend $150 this month). Most of all, be honest with yourself and your friends. Never feel guilty about saying no to an invite.

Missing out on some of the fun is temporary, while going into debt is often a long-term consequence. If your bank account is telling you it's a no-go, don't go.

Pressure to Chip In on Group Gifts

Here Game is very clear. She says: you are the CEO of you. You know how much you make, and how much you spend. When it comes to group giving, don't let the pressure of going over budget tempt you. While your friends will love the gift, you won't love going into debt. Know your numbers and how much you can spend, realistically, of course. If it doesn't fit in with the groups' budget, then buy a separate gift and feel proud for making a good money move. Decline politely. No explanation or apology needed.

If you're the one planning the gift, Richey says to let everyone know the total cost of the item and when you plan to give it, and ask everyone who contributed to sign the card.

Most of all, give from your heart. Your friend who receives the gift will be thrilled no matter what you spent, whether it's part of a group gift or from you alone.

Beware the Financial Frenemies

We all have them. They tell us to "treat ourselves" and that we deserve to reward ourselves by buying something or splurging "for once." Friends that just don't hear us when we gently try to explain that we're on budget. They push us to shop for stuff we don't need. They roll their eyes behind our backs if we express hesitation about a night out that we know will be a budget killer. These are not friends you can afford to keep.

You don't need to have a big breakup scene. Just don't make plans that cost you more than you want to spend. And in return, always be respectful of the financial choices your friends are making.

YOUR FINANCIAL GROWNUP CHECKLIST
∼ FRIENDS ∼

- ✓ Beware: Friends + work can lead to complications.
- ✓ Social media doesn't always mix with business. Be discreet.
- ✓ Friends will have different finances. Be sensitive and kind.
- ✓ Control the bill on group outings.
- ✓ There's nothing romantic about being broke. Date with a financial strategy.
- ✓ Get the budget info before you RSVP to an invitation.
- ✓ Gifts: Give what you want, and don't feel the need to apologize or explain.
- ✓ Dump financial frenemies.

CHAPTER NINE

WEALTH AND WELLNESS

No book on financial independence can avoid addressing the importance of physical and mental health. If you're not healthy, it's going to be very hard to make money, grow your money, and protect your money. Eating healthy foods and staying physically and mentally fit are often mistakenly seen as nice-to-haves – but they're really must-haves. If you're a breadwinner and you get sick you're going to have financial problems. If you get sick or injured and you don't have the right health insurance, you're going to have financial problems. If a dependent, whether it be a parent, child, spouse, or even a pet, gets sick and doesn't have the right insurance, you're going to have financial problems. Even if your computer and other technology devices get "sick," you're going to be exposed to potentially huge financial problems if you're not prepared. Without health and wellness, you have nothing.

ALEXIA BRUE

• PUBLISHER, WELL+GOOD

MY FINANCIAL GROWNUP MOMENT

I was diagnosed with cancer in college. Hodgkin's disease. I had chemotherapy. Usually you deal with your mortality later in life, so it was a real wake-up call. Medical stuff has always been front and center in my life for 20 years. I have lived the cleanest, most healthy life possible since then. Last year I had my second cancer diagnosis. This time breast cancer. It was caught early, and my prognosis is good.

When you have experiences like these, you realize health is not a luxury. It is priceless and a priority.

Well+Good is an extension of my own coming-to-terms with growing up and putting a real financial value on health.

I once read a quote from a very popular female celebrity. She said working out every day was self-indulgent. I think that is wrong. You can do all the right financial planning in life, but if you don't take care of yourself it will cost you everything you have worked so hard to achieve.

MY LESSON TO SHARE

It is about trade-offs. With personal finances there is no way to have it all. You constantly have to prioritize and plan for what's important to you. You can't splurge without saving somewhere else.

I see our Well+Good community employ this principle all the time. Luxury wellness experiences, such as $35 fitness classes and $10 green juices, are expensive, to be sure.

We've seen a lot of our readers re-allocate the way they spend their money. For example, people used to care more about the season's "it" bag or a pair of incredible shoes. Now we see a lot of Millennial women saying to hell with the bag of the season; they'd rather do the workouts they love and splurge on smoothies and green juices.

They've made a conscious trade-off in deciding that these daily experiences mean more to them than a bag. Just think – a $1,500 bag translates into 30 boutique fitness classes and 40 green juices. I can't remember the last time I bought a pricey bag. Instead I've turned my yearly bag splurge into my fitness fund.

INVEST IN YOUR HEALTH – PHYSICAL, MENTAL, TECHNOLOGICAL

WE SAY IT all the time – all that matters is our health. And yet we rarely talk about it as something to invest money in. We'll invest in a statement handbag that will be in style "forever." Or a home renovation. But somehow it seems an indulgent splurge to spend $35 for a boutique fitness class.

To be clear: if you can't afford it, do what you can. But if you're spending on splurge items such as handbags, as Alexia points out, before you invest in the next one make sure it's the best choice.

If you have the money to buy an expensive handbag once a year, or a few pairs of designer shoes, think about what that might buy towards your health in the next year. Probably a nice juicer. Likely a membership to a gym nice enough that you're motivated to go. And don't forget some flattering new workout gear so you feel your best. Give yourself permission to prioritize your health and wellness.

SPEND ON YOUR HEALTH – YOU RELY ON IT EVERY DAY

Health care costs are the biggest cause of bankruptcy, so it's crucial to your financial well-being to stay healthy, and to be ready for the costs when you're not. Here are some stats to really get your heart racing:

- The Consumer Financial Protection Bureau reports that a full 52 percent of credit bureau filings are for medical debt.

- According to NerdWallet, one in five adults struggled to pay medical bills in 2014.

- 1.7 million Americans live in households that will declare bankruptcy because they can't pay medical bills.

- And despite having year-round insurance, 10 million insured Americans ages 19 to 34 will face bills they can't pay, according to NerdWallet.

FOOD FOR THOUGHT

One of our biggest day-to-day expenses is food. But the cost of what we eat is more than a budget item. What we put into our bodies is a key driver of our health, which, as we've shown, has extreme financial consequences. Eating the right foods, bought at the right price, will directly improve your financial health and physical health.

One of the most respected and well-known experts on this topic is Steve Perrine, president of Wolverine Media, Inc., a multimedia company focused on health, nutrition, and fitness and the author of *The New American Diet*. Here are his top suggestions:

When It Comes to Fish, 'tis the Season

For example, Steve says it's worth paying a premium for wild salmon, but not in the winter.

Wild salmon is higher in heart-healthy omega-3 fatty acids and much lower in pesticides and other contaminants. And that nice pink color? In wild salmon, it comes from natural, omega-3-rich feed; in farmed salmon it comes from dyes that are injected into the fish's food pellets to make their flesh appear pink.

But Steve says buyer beware, especially when the temperature drops. A study by the nonprofit organization Oceana found that 43 percent of "wild salmon" sold in stores during winter months is actually farmed salmon. But an earlier study by the same group conducted during summer found that only 7 percent was misla-beled. The reason is that during winter, wild salmon is harder to come by, so mislabeling and fraud are more tempting to fishers and wholesalers.

Steve recommends that you skip the salmon entirely in winter and look for healthier, more-economical sources of omega-3s, especially mackerel and halibut.

Buy Organic – But Not If You Can Peel It

Each year the Environmental Working Group issues its list of the Dirty Dozen most contaminated fruits and vegetables. While this list varies from year to year, Steve says a solid rule of thumb is to buy organic foods when the skins are edible – apples, berries, peppers, lettuce, etc. If it's a food you peel, such as oranges or onions, then paying more for organic is just a waste of money.

Eat More of the Right Peanut Butter

The cheapest health food in the store is probably peanut butter. It's packed with protein, fiber, and healthy fats, which makes it one of the few complete foods out there. But read the ingredients: Steve says that peanut butter should be made of peanuts and maybe a little salt. If it has anything else in it, you're paying money for junk.

Buy Frozen

Frozen fruits and vegetables are picked at peak ripeness and flash-frozen. That means they're probably more nutritious than off-season produce that was picked early and allowed to ripen during its long journey north from Chile. Plus, frozen produce is not only less expensive, it also won't go bad on you.

Pay with Cash

Remember cash? That green stuff that the Tooth Fairy handed out? Consider using it in the grocery store. A study published in the *Journal of Consumer Research* tracked the grocery-shopping habits of 1,000 households over six months and found that shoppers who paid with cash bought fewer processed foods and more nutritious items than those who opted to use credit. The credit users not only spend more on junk, they also spent an average of 59 to 78 percent more on their grocery bills. The explanation: Credit and debit cards are more abstract forms of payment, so you don't use them as carefully as you do cash.

Eat Something Healthy on the Way to the Store

Studies show that people who do that actually make healthier choices once they're inside the supermarket.

Use a Cart, Not a Basket

Many people believe a basket will limit the amount you can carry, hence cutting down your bill. But baskets have the opposite effect: as they get heavier, we begin making less-thoughtful and less-economical choices because we start getting tired and annoyed that we're lugging around this stupid basket. Use a cart and save yourself the hassle, and the expense.

Shop Online – But Wisely

This is one of the best tips I've heard about online shopping. If you like shopping in your bathrobe, great. But do it smartly: Steve says to make a list ahead of time, then use the search box at the top of the webpage to look for your items. You won't get distracted by online aisle browsing.

HEALTH INSURANCE

If your company offers health insurance with your job (or your spouse has it through their employer), that's almost always going to be your best option. The most common types of health care plans are:

- **Health Maintenance Organization plans (HMOs):** You choose a primary care physician from a network of preferred providers (which include doctors, hospitals, and other healthcare professionals) with these plans, and all your health care services go through that doctor (who refers you to specialists in the network should you need one). Visits to providers outside your network are typically not covered, except in an emergency.

- **Preferred Provider Organization plans (PPOs):** You can use any doctor, hospital, and other healthcare provider you choose without a referral with these plans, but there are financial incentives to use providers in the network. Some services may not be available out of network.

- **Point of Service plans (POSs):** These plans, hybrids of HMOs and PPOs, usually require you to choose a primary care physician from within a network of preferred providers, and you need to get referrals to see specialists. These specialists can be out-of-network providers, but there are financial incentives to use providers that are in the network.

- **High-Deductible Health Plans (HDHPs):** These plans can have much more affordable monthly payments, but they often have very high deductibles. They are often paired with health savings accounts, where you contribute pre-tax dollars from your paycheck. That money can be used for medical expenses, such as co-pays and coinsurance that are not covered by your plan. It can also be used for things like dental expenses that may not be covered under your plan. Some employers contribute to HSAs.

Bruce Elliott, manager of compensation and benefits at the Society for Human Resources Management (SHRM), advises signing up for high-deductible plans if you're young and healthy. As you get older, or anticipate higher medical expenses, check out other more appropriate plans during your company's open enrollment period.

He also advises that you research your company's wellness programs. Many of these programs go unused simply because employees aren't aware of them.

Think You May Job Hop?

Elliott recommends considering Health Savings Accounts, because they're portable (you can keep them even if you change jobs). They're also tax-deductible, and if used for qualified medical expenses, such as dental and vision, they're never taxed. HSAs also earn interest, which is also tax-free. Most importantly, the money is yours to keep. That's in contrast to flexible spending accounts (FSAs), which are forfeited at the end of the year.

The Affordable Care Act (a.k.a. Obamacare)

The Affordable Care Act was signed into law in 2010, and it effectively requires all Americans to have health insurance. The plans vary, and information about them is available on Healthcare.gov, which is also where you can apply for coverage.

Perhaps the most important recent change regarding healthcare is that having insurance is no longer optional. Essentially, if you can afford health insurance through the ACA you're mandated to buy it. If you choose to not buy it, there's a penalty fee that you must pay when you file your taxes. If you can't afford health insurance, there are subsidies to help.

The law is still being updated and adjusted, and many groups continue to try to get it changed or eliminated completely. But as long as it's the law, compliance is not optional.

DISABILITY INSURANCE

Your ability to work is your most valuable asset. According to the nonprofit Life Happens, one in four Americans who couldn't work suddenly would have financial problems immediately! They say to think of disability insurance as insurance for your paycheck. Also, according to Life Happens, 61 percent of Americans say most people need disability insurance, and yet only 26 percent have it.

Think honestly about how long you could cover your bills, or your family's bills, if one day you couldn't go to work. There is short-term disability insurance (usually about three months) and long-term disability insurance that kicks in after that. The length of time the long-term disability insurance covers depends on the policy.

Many corporate jobs offer disability insurance as an optional deduction in your paycheck. This is a great option. But be aware of the amount of income it will replace. Generally, it's about 60 percent. Individual policies are available as well, and the percentage of your salary that they replace will vary according to the policy you choose.

There are calculators on websites like Life Happens to help you figure out your needs and to make the best choice. One last stat to motivate you: three in ten people will be out of work for 90 days or more because of a disability, according to Life Happens.

LIFE INSURANCE

If you are single and don't have dependents, you may not think you need life insurance. And you may not. But think carefully about what would happen if you were to pass away. Have your parents co-signed loans? What happens to your student debt? As morbid as it may sound, your family will also have expenses, like funeral costs and legal bills to contend with. So before you dismiss the idea of life insurance, give it some thought.

If you have a family, don't think about it, do it. You need life insurance. The only question is how much and how fast you can get it if it's not already in place. Many employers offer some coverage, so that's a good place to start. In most cases, you'll want to add to that coverage personally. Your needs are unique, so do the homework and get it done. The sooner you do it, the lower the premiums are likely to be – so get going!

PET INSURANCE

Pets are family. And their health is priceless. I can't think of a single person I know who wouldn't spend every penny asked of them to save their pet's life, or to provide comfort when they're in pain. But the financial reality of that love and committment is huge.

The Best Birthday Present for a New Pet

Wendy Diamond, founder of Animal Fair, is a big advocate for pet insurance.

She says that if you have a young and healthy pet then it can seem a waste of money to be paying health insurance. In fact, this is just the time that you should be making the purchase. Monthly premiums can be as low as $20 in the case of a young healthy dog, depending on the coverage you decide on.

It's also worth noting that most pet insurance policies don't cover existing conditions – another reason to insure your pet while it's still young and healthy. Some companies even allow you to lock the premiums at a set amount for the lifetime of your dog. You'll have to pay extra for this, but it may be worth it.

For instance, if your pet belongs to a large dog breed it can be more susceptible to hip dysplasia. This can be treated but it's going to cost – if you already have insurance in place this can help. If you've locked in your premiums then they won't increase with diagnosis.

Types of Pet Insurance

There are two types of pet insurance – accident and comprehensive.

Accident insurance provides for care should your pet encounter a misfortune, such as severe cuts and bruises suffered when it decides to be a little too adventurous and falls down a hole.

Comprehensive pet insurance covers all health eventualities, such as cancer, which is responsible for 50 percent of disease-related animal deaths annually. Comprehensive insurance is the most popular with pet parents, with approximately 95 percent of people who insure their pets choosing this option. Most companies allow you to modify your policy so that you can alter the size of premiums – for instance, by changing the amount of deductible you have to pay.

There are also wellness plans available, says Diamond. Wellness plans are not actually insurance; they provide a certain amount of coverage for the day-to-day medical care of your pet, including routine check-ups.

Wendy's warning: *Don't think that, as an alternative to insurance, you can just save every month in a pet's version of a health savings account.*

Many people might feel that they would rather put money into an account to provide for pet emergencies. Wendy says that that may be a very good idea for ongoing veterinary costs, such as payment for check-ups. But what happens if something unexpected happens and you have to pay thousands of dollars for an operation for your dog? You're unlikely to have saved that much money, especially if you've only been saving for a few months. If you have pet insurance in place, this can help with the cost.

Do your homework, just like with any big financial decision.

There are several pet insurance providers and different kinds of policies, so it's a good idea to check out sites such as Consumers Advocate and Pet Insurance Review for a bit of independent information when you're looking for an insurance policy. Remember, it's always best to take out a policy while your pet is young and healthy. Then, depending on the coverage you choose, you'll be able to have your pet treated and claim a refund on the cost.

You may not think that that happy, healthy pet in your home will ever need an operation, but you don't know what's around the corner, and having pet insurance can provide some peace of mind.

TECHNOLOGY HEALTH

We may joke about our dependence on technology, but it's a big part of every aspect of our lives. Keeping our information secure is extremely important and a big challenge. It only takes one weak link in the chain to bring down major corporations or ruin personal finances. A survey done by MasterCard showed that a majority of people would rather have nude photos of themselves leaked online than have their financial data compromised.

And yet, 46 percent of the survey respondents rarely, if ever, changed their passwords. And as you'll read, even if they did they would still be vulnerable.

Actions Need to Speak Louder than Words

Palo Alto Networks CEO Mark McLaughlin is one of the leading experts on cybersecurity and keeping your technology healthy and safe. Here are Mark's Top 5 Cyber Hygiene Lessons:

- **Social media doesn't have a back button.** Despite that little arrow at the top of your browser, once something goes out into the Internet, it should be considered permanent. This is one of the most repeated digital idioms, but we still regularly see information posted to social media that's a primary resource for attackers. From a cybersecurity standpoint, it's important to limit the personal information you put online that could make you a target. A common hacking technique involves learning about a target's personal life, job, and interests from social media, and then using this information to reset passwords and take over email or banking accounts.

- **Password 2.0.** This brings me to my next lesson: most passwords we create are ineffective at stopping hacks. Despite our best attempts, when we make passwords that we need to remember, we tend to fall back on what we know. This leaves users vulnerable to the social engineering of passwords based on public information (see Lesson 1). A couple of strategies you can use to help evolve your password are: two-factor authentication, which provides you with a randomized code every time you log in; and a password manager, which can create and remember multiple complex passwords so you don't have to. Both of these technologies add an extra layer of security to your sensitive accounts and are easy to set up and use.

- **Leaky clouds.** Even with strong passwords we can sometimes be our own worst enemy. Cloud applications and storage, such as iCloud, Google Drive, and DropBox, have brought cheap, on-demand storage to the mass market, storing everything from personal photos to important documents and files. In fact, Palo Alto's annual Application Usage and Threat Report shows that the use of cloud applications among their customers has exploded nearly 50 percent since 2012, and it now includes over 316 different types of apps. Because of the popularity of these apps, many employees end up using their personal accounts to share work files. If sharing and privacy settings are misconfigured, you risk accidentally sharing your corporate product roadmap outside your company. Corporations now have options to secure the use of approved cloud applications, or lock down the use of personal accounts, but it's up to everyone to focus on good cybersecurity.

- **Gone phishing.** Personal responsibility is critically important for good cybersecurity at work and for your own protection.

Spear phishing email messages prey on a lack of attention and awareness, by tricking users into opening malicious attachments or clicking dangerous links. How big of a problem is spear phishing? Palo Alto found that, among their customer base, over 40 percent of email attachments that they analyzed were malicious. While many security technologies today work to filter spear phishing messages, or neutralize their malicious attachments and links, the only way to be sure they can't infect you is by not falling for them. Being aware of suspicious email, and thinking before you click, is the most important line of defense.

- **Stay cyber-savvy.** Finally, and most importantly, stay educated and maintain awareness about threats to your data and privacy. On average Palo Alto has seen a six-hour gap between when a story about a new threat hits the news and when it's widely used against their customers. When new threats hit the mainstream media, pay attention to the implications for your own privacy and data security. Ultimately you're responsible for what happens to your data, and that data could affect your personal life, finances, and even your job.

As our personal and professional lives become more and more digital, it's the responsibility of all of us to work to prevent successful cyberattacks. By staying cyber-savvy and following a few basic tips, you can prevent damaging attacks and help preserve our digital way of life.

If You Crash Don't Get Burned

You should first back up everything on all your devices to something physical, such as a hard drive. But remember, hard drives can also crash and break; it's happened to me. Sometimes the data can be recovered, but sometimes it can't, and it's often expensive to try.

Next you should back up to the cloud. There are a lot of free services available such as iCloud, Google, Dropbox, Box, and so on. Depending on how much data you need to back up, you may want to pay for more storage. I find that paying for the premium version of these services is often money well spent because of the added functionality. I use Dropbox and have been very happy with it. Photos on my phone are automatically sent up to my Dropbox account, so I never have to panic if my phone goes missing. Whatever service you choose, make sure to take the time to set it up properly so you have everything automated.

Know Thy Neighbors

We're all a little too trusting when it comes to WiFi. Recent data from MasterCard showed that more than half of Millennials go online in public places to check financial information. That's naive. Don't do it unless you really know who is controlling that WiFi connection.

Embrace Change

Most people don't. Remember this stat: Close to half of all Americans rarely change passwords. And that's not counting the many people who use the same passwords for multiple accounts (I'm guilty there!). If you're like me, you change your passwords and then forget what you chose and have to change them again. It's a vicious cycle!

Changing your passwords regularly limits how long a stolen password is useful to the thief – how long he or she has access to your account. But changing passwords every 30 to 180 days can become burdensome, especially if you need a lot of passwords. One option is to use a password management site such as Dashlane or Lastpass. Both offer a lot of free services. For example, Lastpass will notify you if it looks like one of your accounts is hacked. Plus, Dashlane offers access to your accounts in an emergency. If something happens to you, and a loved one needs to get into your accounts, that's one less hassle they need to worry about.

Hopefully you will never spill coffee on your computer, have your phone fall into the water, or leave your tablet in a taxi. But taking care of your devices and online accounts will help to protect you if technology tragedy strikes.

GET ORGANIZED

Organizing your clutter is good for your health. The average American owns more possessions than our brains evolved to handle. If you think back to the days of the hunter/gatherer, all that early humans had were the loincloths on their bodies and maybe a tool or two. Now people can have a thousand items in a kitchen alone. Clutter makes it difficult to relax both physically and mentally.

Recent studies of how the human brain's visual cortex processes multiple visual stimuli found that the more clutter there is in sight, the less productive you are. The bottom line is that an organized physical space creates an organized mental space, allowing more clarity of thought and increased creativity.

So how do you eliminate the clutter that surrounds you?

Organization expert Barbara Reich suggests that you ask yourself these questions.

- Is the item in good condition, or can it be repaired? *If the answer is no, say goodbye.*

- Have I used the item in the last year? Past behavior is the best indicator of future behavior. *If the answer is no, say goodbye.*

- Will I ever use it again? *If the answer is no, say goodbye.*

- Am I holding on to something I hate only because someone I love gave it to me? *If the answer is yes, say goodbye.*

- If I discard the item and find I need it later, is it replaceable? *If the answer is yes, say goodbye.*

Organize Your Bills

Losing stuff is expensive – piles of envelopes with bills can go unpaid, and money-related emails can go unopened.

Being organized is financially smart. When you're organized you don't waste time looking for things (and time is money!). You pay your bills on time, thus avoiding interest payments and a falling credit score.

Barbara Reich suggests having both a place to put unpaid bills and a routine for paying them. For example, an inbox on your desk or a digital folder on your computer can hold bills and items that can't be taken care of at the moment. Then designate a time each week when you'll review the information and pay those bills.

Don't Forget Your Digital Files

Digital organization with respect to finances can be a huge time-saver. While many people pay bills online and get other financial information online, they overlook the filing of these documents. Just as you would create paper files for documents, create files on your computer. Reich says to make sure that you periodically review statements and don't just file them to empty your in-box. A messy computer doesn't assault the eye the way a messy desk does, but it can get in the way of an organized life even more since we rely on it for so many tasks.

Take Subscriptions Off Autopilot

We all sign up for things that we believe we'll use, and we often set up recurring monthly, quarterly, or yearly renewals. This is great when it comes to things like making deposits into our retirement accounts. But not so much with stuff we may no longer need.

It may be apps, subscriptions to magazines, gym memberships, or other monthly recurring charges that hit our credit cards or checking accounts without us blinking an eye. What we rarely do is deliberately comb through our bills, assess which services we continue to use, and then cancel the ones we don't. Take the time, at least once a year, to go through everything that hits your finances automatically. Then make the call to cancel anything you're no longer using. You may even realize that you're paying for something you do want to use, and now you'll be reminded to start using it. There are even services out there that will do this for you, such as Trim, which tracks your credit card recurring charges and alerts you to subscriptions that you're no longer using.

ONE FINAL THOUGHT: CLEAR YOUR THOUGHTS

Some of the most successful people in the world embrace meditation and mindfulness. Studies have shown that many of the benefits of meditation, including lower stress levels and better focus, directly improve one's health and in turn lower the cost of healthcare. Best of all, meditation is free. There are lots of great meditation apps out there. I'm a fan of Headspace and Calm. Both have valuable features available for free, and subscription plans if you want to get more content.

*Constantly prioritize and plan
for what's important to you*

YOUR FINANCIAL GROWNUP CHECKLIST
∼ HEALTH ∼

- Focus on being healthy in order to be wealthy.

- Health is priceless, most "stuff" isn't.

- Watch your food costs – both financial and health.

- Get health insurance, and don't get penalized.

- Uncover "hidden" wellness benefits.

- You are not invincible. Get disability and life insurance.

- Insure your pets.

- Practice safe and secure technology healthcare.

- Organize to stay on top of finances.

- Meditate to lower healthcare costs and boost productivity.

CHAPTER TEN

EDUCATE YOURSELF, THEN OTHERS

Thanks to the Internet you now have infinite resources to educate yourself when it comes to your money. There's no shortage of mortgage calculators and web resources to figure out budgets, tax planning, etc. There are endless self-help articles and videos on how to set up a business, get a raise, save money, and be healthier. But they won't help unless you decide to use them and then invest the time to figure out what works for you.

A number of people that suggested that I use scare tactics to motivate you to pay attention to your money. For the most part I've avoided that. But the truth is, not having money is danger-ous and scary. The old idea of the glamourous starving artist is a bunch of you-know-what. You need money. It's your responsibility to earn and maintain money for yourself and for your family. Be-ing a Financial Grownup isn't a choice – it's a mandate. Just ask Jim Cramer.

JIM CRAMER

- HOST, CNBC'S *MAD MONEY*
- CO-FOUNDER, THESTREET.COM

MY FINANCIAL GROWNUP MOMENT

My financial grownup moment was when I lost everything in a series of robberies in Los Angeles and, when I came back from covering a sniper in San Diego for the now-defunct *L.A. Herald Examiner,* I was evicted from my apartment and was homeless. Nothing like homelessness to concentrate the mind and make you realize that it was time to go make some money. I never wanted to be poor again and went from journalism to finance, working my way from my car to sales and trading at Goldman Sachs in four years' time.

MY LESSON TO SHARE

Money is a necessary evil. I didn't realize it until my house and my bank account were emptied by someone who was never caught by the police, and all I had were the clothes on my back and my 1978 Ford Fairmont. Once I had a taste of horrific poverty I recognized that I had to find a way to claw back from being down, and I set my sights on it and would not be denied the opportunity to prosper. Fortunately, getting off the canvas in this great country is not as hard as it would seem. And while I certainly did some damage to my body during those hard-fought days – you stay warm in your car with a bottle of Jack – I learned the tough way that, like a variant on that old Dunkin Donuts ad, it was time to make the money.

BECOME FINANCIALLY LITERATE

MONEY ISN'T ABOUT being materialistic. As Jim says, it's a necessary evil. Money can be a tool to achieve your dreams. That's the upside. But the downside is a very serious one.

More than half of people in the United States have no rainy-day funds, according to the FINRA Investor Education Foundation (Financial Industry Regulatory Authority, 2012). That means they're putting themselves in the same precarious position Jim Cramer was in. If you're single, that's irresponsible. If you're responsible for someone else, such as a child or an older family member, it's dangerous and unacceptable.

> *Money is a necessary evil*

Poverty is increasing among retirees. Depending on social security is naive. No one will be there to save you when you can't pay your mortgage or a big health bill.

America is in a personal finance crisis, and Americans are in denial. According to at 2014 Harris poll conducted for the National Foundation for Credit Counseling (NFCC), only 39 percent of adults even have a budget or keep track of their spending.

In other words, a significant majority of adults, 61 percent, aren't even keeping track of what they spend. How could they possibly be financial grownups?

It gets worse: That same survey found that about one in three U.S. adults still don't save any of their household's annual income.

About one in three U.S. adults (34 percent) indicated that their household carries credit card debt from month to month.

Financial literacy is rarely taught in schools. As the United States moves away from corporations taking care of their employees, we do little to educate Americans about the financial challenges they may face. It's no surprise that, according to PwC, only 24 percent of young adults ages 23 to 34 demonstrate basic financial knowledge.

Health insurance, long provided by employers, could soon see a major shift as The Affordable Care Act continues to evolve. Even if an employer does provide and subsidize insurance, it's up to employees to know what they're entitled to, and to be prepared for the likely changes to come.

Investing has become a minefield for the average investor. Mutual funds may tout fantastic returns, but many of the fees can be hidden. As we discussed earlier in the book, even 401(k)s are loaded with fees! But staying on the sidelines isn't an option. Investing still remains the best option. Smart investors will be strategic and make deliberate, well-thought-out decisions.

And that brings us to our final Role Model. Tony Robbins came from nothing and now inspires millions to take control of their lives. His book *Money: Master the Game* continues to be a bestseller in large part because of its no-excuses mantra. His most important message: Take care of yourself, then give.

TONY ROBBINS

- BEST-SELLING AUTHOR AND ENTREPRENEUR

MY FINANCIAL GROWNUP MOMENT

We had no money for food at Thanksgiving. That will kind of wake you up. But what it woke me up to was not only that I wanted to do well financially so my future family would not suffer the way we did. Somebody fed my family. So it also, at the same time, made me incredibly grateful, and it made me believe that strangers care. It wasn't about the food, it was about the fact that somebody cared. And I swore that I would do that for somebody else, so when I was 17 I fed two families. The next year four. And as years went by I did hundreds of thousands. And in the last seven years, it's been two million people through my foundation. And then I fed two million, so that is four million total. And then with this book I just did, *Money: Master the Game,* we are feeding 100 million people. I am feeding 50 million people myself through Feeding America and then I'm doing matching funds to reach 100 million people. So you can be imprinted by some of the earliest things in your life.

MY LESSON TO SHARE

I would say the most important thing is stop being a consumer. Become an owner. You know you have to. You might say: I don't have time to invest, I don't know what investing is. It seems so complex. But if you don't study just a couple of basic things and really learn to own the companies, not just buy from

> *Stop being a consumer –
> become an owner*

panies, not just buy from these companies, then you are always going to struggle financially. You can move from being the chess piece to the chess player, and there are a few distinctions you really need to know. And that is what I have really worked on sharing with people.

———

SHARE

SHARING HE does. All the proceeds from Tony's book are being donated to Feeding America through his 100 Million Meals Challenge.

GIVER BEWARE

Giving is a big part of being a financial grownup. But we have to cover one important part of giving, and that is: giver beware. Just as you have to carefully screen who you work with, and who you trust to invest your money, you must do your homework when it comes to charity.

First, make sure the charity is legitimate. There are many websites, such as Charity Navigator and GuideStar, that can help you confirm that a charity is what it says it is. Be sure to look at how much of the money they raise actually goes to the cause you're supporting. Some charities have bloated administrative costs, such as high salaries for executives. They also sometimes spend a lot of money on fancy benefit events and celebrity appearances, and then have little left to put toward their cause.

CASH IS (SOMETIMES) KING

Recently some savvy charities have moved away from lavish events. DonorsChoose.org, which allows donors to give directly to classroom projects, for example, doesn't have an actual benefit, where some of the proceeds would go to expenses for that event.

Donating is also a financially savvy move for the giver. Donations to 501(c)3 charities, such as DonorsChoose.org, are tax-deductible to the full extent of U.S. law. That's great news come tax time. Both you and the charity will have more money – it's a win-win.

Time is money, so giving your time and hands-on effort is a great way to support a charity. But giving money should never be thought of as second best. Many young, idealistic people say they want to work in a low-paying, non-profit job because they want to create a better world. That's wonderful. But going to work in a high-paying job, or building a company that creates jobs, can be equally and in many cases more effective. Think of all the billionaires, such as Bill and Melinda Gates and Mark Zuckerberg and his wife Priscilla Chan, who make a difference in the world with their generosity.

But it's not just billionaires or even millionaires – it's all of us. Every dollar makes a tangible difference. For example, at DonorsChoose.org $5 could help buy those last few paint brushes for an art project; $50 could help furnish some new chemistry lab supplies; $500 might add another laptop or tablet to a classroom; and $5,000 could help students travel to Asia to learn about international business.

As you can see, while going into the class and helping would be great, in some cases it *is* about the money.

PAY IT FORWARD

Please give the gift of financial literacy. Some proceeds from this book will be going to support DonorsChoose.org. The organization, founded by Role Model Charles Best, has received the highest rating by Charity Navigator every year since 2005. You can find projects at www.donorschoose.org/financialgrownup to give specifically to financial literacy, but there are incredible projects that are in need in all areas, so please explore the rest of the site as well.

BE TRUE TO YOURSELF

Helping others is also a priority for our last Role Model: actor and businesswoman Drew Barrymore. Her efforts to support others include a $1 million donation to the World Food Programme, and working as an Ambassador Against Hunger.

At the age of six Drew was thrust into a very grownup world as the breakout star of Steven Spielberg's *E.T.* I met Drew at an event in New York City, where she spoke about her ups and downs as an actor and her journey building her businesses. Drew was quite candid about the tough financial decisions she made over the course of her career, both as an actor and as a businesswoman. I was able to chat with her privately after the event, and she generously shared this story.

DREW BARRYMORE

- FOUNDER, FLOWER BEAUTY
- FOUNDER, FLOWER FILMS
- ACTOR

MY FINANCIAL GROWNUP MOMENT

My financial grownup moment was being told by Steven Spielberg to turn down money. This was after *E.T.* and I was getting all kinds of endorsement offers. And for many years afterwards it was very difficult because I would have liked to have that money and maybe even needed that money very much. But in the end it – pun intended – paid off because I was able to learn about integrity and that working for your money is not only key and crucial, but if you haven't spread yourself too thin you probably will have better opportunities later. Even if they are the ones only created from yourself, you won't have confused everyone along the way.

MY LESSON TO SHARE

I think that when you have the intention of wanting to strike it rich something might possibly go awry, and if you pour your heart into something and you know that one day you might have enough to support yourself, that is literally the energy that has to go into building whatever it is you are trying to build.

GET HELP FROM OTHERS

DREW HAD BEEN offered quite a few lucrative endorsement deals after *E.T.* She could have cashed in, but she didn't go for the quick, easy hit. She was thoughtful, and she had a long-range plan that has paid off. Drew wanted to control her identity, what we now call her personal brand, and not simply sell it to the highest bidder.

She runs her own production company, Flower Films, and has a makeup line at Walmart called Flower Beauty, which will soon expand its online and international presence. I met some of her business partners and it's clear that she surrounds herself with smart, business-savvy, experienced people. Drew learned early on that, while ultimately you must be your own financial grownup, getting help and advice from people who are willing and able to help is the secret weapon of many financially successful people.

That was the mission of this book: To bring you advice from highly successful people who were willing to share their stories. Learn from the experiences and advice of the Role Models and experts here. Take what you can from them, and then tailor it to fit your financial goals. Dealing with money can be messy. There's no one size fits all. But there are experiences that we all share.

You are now ready to be a financial grownup.

CONCLUSION

YOUR OWN GROWNUP MOMENT

I F YOU HAVEN'T HAD IT ALREADY, you will soon. That moment when you realize that if you don't pay attention to money, you will never have the financial freedom to live your dreams.

Take the stories from the Role Models in this book, and the advice from the experts, and use it to make mindful decisions about your adult financial life. Pay attention to the way the people around you deal with money. Learn from the ones who are successful, and from those who make mistakes. Don't be afraid to talk about it. Some of the best advice you will get may come from candid conversations that evolve just because you asked.

People are often more generous than you would expect when you simply talk to them about their experiences.

This book became real when I made an appointment to talk to the President and Editor-in-Chief of Reuters, Steve Adler. I barely knew him. But in addition to heading Reuters, he was a bestselling author with a new book out. The poor guy probably had no idea what was about to hit him when he agreed to meet with me. I asked him everything I could think of about getting a book published. But he sat patiently and kept answering my questions. He liked the concept and told me to get going and write the book already. And so I did.

If you want to learn how to do something, ask someone who is good at it to tell you their story. Apply that to everything in your life, not just money, and you will go far.

ACKNOWLEDGEMENTS

Financial Grownup was truly a passion project for me but it was a group effort to bring it to all of you!

I can't thank Jim Pennypacker and the team at Maven House enough for all their support. I feel truly blessed to have a publisher that believed in my vision for a new approach to self help/personal finance. You set a high bar, and it shows. Big kudos as well to the folks at Perseus/Legato, including Jeff Tegge and Mark Hillesheim who did a great job creating initial buzz for the project, and following through with early sales success.

Tony Robbins for the wonderful foreward and enthusiastic participation in Financial Grownup. When I started this project, I had one big name at the top of my wish list: Tony Robbins. Like so many people, I had every excuse in the book not to write a book: a full time job, raising a family and a million other things going on. But Tony motivated me, as he has millions, to get over those excuses. Tony- when I asked you to contribute to the book, you immediately smiled and told me what a great idea it was, and that the time had come for something like this. I knew at that moment, if Tony believed in it, this was going to be something special. Tony, you are my role model.

The heart and soul of this book are the incredible Financial Grownup Role Models who generously shared their personal stories and advice. Thank you for opening up your lives to our readers, and being so candid about life's financial adventures. It is truly a gift that will impact countless lives.

I am also in debt to the phenomenal team of experts who provided the solutions to so many life challenges that we all face as financial grownups. I came to all of you with long lists of questions, and you were there with the answers.

Adam Kirschner you were there with me from the beginning, including a number of false starts. But you stuck with me. Along with the formidable Jen Ashkenazy, you believed in the concept from day one, and helped make it happen. I look forward to a long and successful partnership.

Claudio Marinesco thank you for the fantastic photo that graces the cover of this book. Your incredible talent is only matched by your sense of humor and charming personality.

All Good NYC- Nick Johnson and Gabe Zimmer thank you not only for a great website but for your infinite patience!

Reuters has been my home for the majority of my career and it would take an entire book to thank everyone who has helped me along the way. Financial Grownup literally may not have happened if Steve Adler had not been so encouraging when I came to him with the concept. Dan Colarusso, thank you for giving me a hard time at first- making it that much better when you came around! Lauren Young, Beth Pinsker and Chris Taylor and honorable mention to Linda Stern- thank you for taking me under your wings and making me an honorary member of the money team. Marie Frail, your infinite patience with all my side hustles will always be appreciated. Conway Gittens, for always being a cheerleader even when I drove you nuts. Aleks Michalska, for picking up the pieces when I needed an extra hand. Fred Katayama for all those times you switched duties with me so I could race out for a book-related meeting. David Gaffen for all the great book advice. The social media team led by Cassandra Garrison who always give my stories that extra kick. Alex Cohen and Leah Duncan - forever grateful for your enthusiasm. The entire tech team led by Jamie Weber, Ross Sholder and Andrew D'Antonio who always have my back. Reuters PR Abbe Serphos, Marina Lopes along with ethics editor Alix Freedman: thank you for allowing me the privilege of representing Reuters in the media, and for your support of this project. And the wizards/therapists in hair and makeup led by Tonia Ciccone. Leah Stangas, Paula Rivera, Adrienne Vazquez: You not only make me look a whole lot better each day you make each day better.

Jenn Connelly, Terri Kayden and the entire JConnelly team: You believed in this book well before I was a client. Your creativity, resourcefulness, attention to detail and all around positive energy has been priceless. I am so fortunate to have you in my corner.

To the RSS Mom Squad: You know who you are. Special mention to Jennifer Wolff, Jill Kasner, Ellyssa Friedland, Dara Freed, Marcy Barkan, Jenna Segal, Jan Schillay, Dara Weiss, Sandy Yoraschek, Nadia Gold, Viviane Silvera Newman, Jessica Weiser, Deb Kroll-Mandel, Jen Russell, Niccole Kroll, Dina Bakst, Erica Keswin, Alexia Brue, Marlene Baron, Allyson Goldstein, Ghena Korn, Jamie Kohen, Erina Polovets, Mitchie Topper, Judi Rimerman, Karen Orzechowski, Deborah Slade, Laura Stuken, Lisa Kalish, Tamar Avnet, Amy Fridman, Jennifer Lotke, Felicia Nachman, Shira

Ronen, Amity Dayan, Alison Ambeault, Jasmine Rothbard, Natalie Silverstein, Lauren Wolfson, Betty Margolin, Robin Kranich, and Juju Chang. Thank you for being the ultimate cheerleaders, listeners and most of all - connectors. Whoever says women don't support women hasn't met this group.

Infinite thanks to so many friends, mentors, and colleagues who have supported and advised me on both this project and over the years including Erika Miller Greff, Allison Weiss Brady, Laura Rowley, Caroline Shapiro, Jeanne Yurman, Pam Samuels Bar, Elizabeth Koraca Harris, Stacy Schneider, Elizabeth Gerst, Francesca Segre, Samira Nanda Sine, Dana Albert, Amy and Ben Rand, Alex Fitzsimons, Davia Temin, Susie Gharib, Jackie Reses, Syma Sambar, Susan Correa, Heidi Gardner, Leigh Goldman, Joya Dass, Jane King, Scott Wenger, Shartia Brantley, Adam Schaffner, Steven Weiss, Caroline Waxler, Helaine Olen, Ron Lieber Jack Doran, Ed Caldwell, Megan Disciullo, Shannon Schuyler, Mitch Roschelle, Jean Chatzsky, Andy Serwer, Jared Blikre, Alexis Christophorous, Rick Newman, Nicole Sinclair, Justine Underhill, Kelly Carty, Janis Cecil, Sasha Salama, Stacy Ostow, Brooke Effron, Johanna Berkman, Sasha Salama, Althea Thompson and Robin Dolch.

My amazing and supportive book club. Ironically the writing of this book meant way too many missed meetings- but you have all been there cheering me on for years and offering great advice. Val, Melissa, Marcy, Tori, Erika, Felice, Loryn, and Jenni - thank you.

To my incredible family including my amazing aunts: Margie, Carol, Phyllis and Sharon. My late mother, Adele Rebell, would be so proud to see how you have all been by my side whenever I needed you, and so much more. She always said the most important thing is to show up, and you do. Thank you also to all of my uncles and cousins with special mention to Janelle Lin Immerman and Dave Kovall for their support of Financial Grownup.

The best siblings ever. Lifetime cheerleaders and best friends. Deb and Jon thank you for everything. Jason, Noah for being amazing brother-in-laws. And my fabulous nephew Asher and niece Sienna.

Ed and Monica your smiles are endless. Thank your for embracing me from day one. And to the rest of the Kaufman crew: Rhonda, Lisa, Ben, Jacob and Noah. And Marc, Madeline, Daniel, Lauren and Brian. I also want to thank the newest members of my family, including my stepmother Susan and all of her kids: Andrew and Crystal (and Ollie!), Greg and Jessica, Josh and Katrina, and Allison.

To my father (and uncredited but always appreciated real estate advisor!), Arthur Rebell, who let me know it was ok to fail, but has always been there with me to celebrate success. I hope I made you proud.

To my husband Neil, there are no words to express my endless gratitude for your love and support. As hours, days and weeks spent on this project turned into months and eventually a couple of years, you have been there by my side. I promise I'll take a break - soon.

And finally to our children and future financial grownups, Ashley, Bradley and Harry. This book is ultimately for you. I know when you read it you will learn something about money. But I hope you will also learn something about your stepmother/mother, and about setting your sights on a goal, and going for it. Believe in yourself first, and others will follow.

INDEX

ABOUT THE AUTHOR

BOBBI REBELL is an award-winning journalist and advocate for financial literacy. She currently leads the U.S. business video unit for Reuters, the largest news organization in the world. In that role she anchors business reports, interviews top newsmakers, and reports on breaking news. Her work is syndicated globally and seen by millions of viewers on Reuters broadcast and online clients. Bobbi also writes a globally syndicated personal finance column on millennials.

Bobbi's work has appeared on countless media outlets including Reuters, Fox, CNBC, CNN, *NYTimes.com*, *WSJ.com*, *MSN.com*, *Yahoo Finance*, *Huffington Post*, *USA Today*, *Time.com*, *Money.com*, *NYPost.com*, PBS, and many more. She began her business news career as an intern at CNN, where she worked with top journalists including Maria Bartiromo, Lou Dobbs, and Stuart Varney. Her first job was at CNBC, after which she went on to work at CNN and Nightly Business Report.

Bobbi is a graduate of the University of Pennsylvania. She holds a Certificate in Financial Planning from New York University. She lives in New York City with her husband, their son, her teenage stepkids, and morkie Waffles.